THEATRE OF DREAMS

A LIFETIME OF DEVOTION TO MANCHESTER UNITED

CHRIS MOORE

This book is dedicated to my parents, who saw me launched in life with love and commitment. To Billy my father and Kathleen my mother (who died on 7 October 1996 at 5.07 pm, just five minutes after the arrival from England of my eldest son Jason, her first grandchild) thanks for the opportunity of growing up in a loving environment and for giving me the strength to face life's unpredictable path.

Chris Moore, January 1997

First published in 1997 by
Marino Books
16 Hume Street Dublin 2
Trade enquiries to CMD Distribution
55A Spruce Avenue Stillorgan Industrial
Park Blackrock County Dublin

© Chris Moore 1997

ISBN 1 86023 060 1

10 9 8 7 6 5 4 3 2 1

A CIP record for this title is available
from the British Library

Cover photograph by the author
Cover design by Penhouse Design
Set by Richard Parfrey
Printed in Ireland by ColourBooks,
Baldoyle Industrial Estate, Dublin 13

CONTENTS

INTRODUCTION

From no Roy Keane to 'Who the fuck are FC Porto?' Ninety minutes of sheer joy, of awesome football that defied belief, even logic. Four nil! Incredible. A night to live in the memory. Our finest hour in Europe since 1968 when we stuffed Portugal's then champions Benfica 4–1 in the European Cup final at Wembley. The date was 5 March 1997. The location was the Theatre of Dreams. And our mission was to conquer Europe to begin the process of catching up with the Scousers' record of four European Cup final victories.

FC Porto came to Old Trafford with a fearsome European record and most of our opponents firmly believed that this match would end our interest in Europe. In truth, even we supporters feared its potential to be the worst. As we stood inside the ground moments before kick-off, the chatter was about not having Keane to run midfield, of trying to neutralise their attack and perhaps sneak one goal at the other end. We recognised that we really needed two goals to be in with a chance of securing our place in the European Champions Cup semi-finals. But when Giggs tucked away a superb third goal against Porto, we were so relaxed we felt confident enough to enquire of the Portuguese fans tucked away in one high corner of the stands, 'Are you City in disguise?'

Life's road is marked with memories – ups and downs, the good, the bad and the ugly: the first time you had sex, the exhilaration of achievement in studies or in the workplace, the day you got married/divorced, family births, deaths and marriages, the day JFK died, the day a team died at Munich. But unlike the assassination of President Kennedy in Dallas, the Manchester United air disaster at Munich on 6 February 1958 was not one of those far distant events which remains in one's consciousness solely because of its historical impact. Munich was made personal for me by my Uncle Bobby's friendship with Harry Gregg, the United goalkeeper at the time. The brief moments of fear for Harry's survival, then the joy and relief of discovering that he was still alive set me off on a lifetime of devotion to the greatest club football side in the world – a lifetime of discovery, of painful disappointments, but also of delight and sheer ecstasy.

It all began when I was seven and has lasted beyond the twenty-six years of Liverpool's dominance, the years of longing for a League Championship title and witnessing a succession of managers unable to match Matt Busby's gloriously successful sides of the 1950s and 1960s. The Busby Babes died in Munich, but by the FA Cup final of 1963 Busby had recovered from the appalling injuries he suffered in the crash and begun to assemble a second team to storm to the top of British football. Denis Law's first goal in that 3-1 win over Leicester City marked the beginning of one hour's total ecstasy – a sexless orgasm. It was almost too much for a twelve-year-old to take. I played every ball, made every tackle, endured the pain of their tackles and took every free kick, throw-in and corner, from the discomfort of my armchair.

Supporting Manchester United has been a journey of extremes – the stomach knotted as we stared at the lost points of a draw or even worse, a defeat, with minutes to go before full-time, then a Charlton shot from twenty-five yards, a Best dribble round the opposition before slipping the ball into the net, a Law scissors kick, a Cantona volley or a Beckham free, or that famous Hughes volley at Wembley which in one split second rescued the first Double of the Double Double. Ecstasy! Then at other times in abject misery you must listen to others gloat over your suffering. Winning and losing, life and death. You give your all for the team.

Theatre of Dreams is the story of one man's journey through life as a born-again, prepared to bleed red, white and black, Manchester United supporter.

> We are just one of those teams that you see now
>   and then,
> We often score six, but seldom score ten,
> We beat them at home, we beat them away,
> We kill any bastards who get in our way.
>
> We are the pride of all Europe, the cock of the
>   north,
> We hate the Scousers – and Cockneys of course (and
>   Leeds),
> We are United without a doubt, we are the
>   Manchester boys!

Part I

The Glorious Sixties

1

THEATRE OF DREAMS

This was my 'everyone-knows-what-they-were-doing-when-President-Kennedy-was-shot' moment. It was 1958 and I was at home in Ballymoney, County Antrim, a market town with a population of just a few thousand. Our house was about a mile outside the town on the road to Dunloy. On the day in question I could do little but look on in bewilderment as *they* huddled in a corner of our living room, talking in whispers – adult stuff not meant for the ears of a seven-year-old. Clearly something dreadful had happened, and the hint of tears from my Uncle Bobby confirmed my worst suspicions.

He was my first hero and role model, Uncle Bobby Brolly, my mother's brother. He was a footballer who had played for Derry City in two Irish cup finals and who finished his career with Cliftonville, the only 'amateur' team in the league at the time. I'd once seen him play for amateur Ireland at Coleraine Showgrounds against a team in red – so it could have been Wales or Spain or Switzerland. My greatest pleasure in visiting his house was to gaze lovingly at the international caps in his cabinet. He's in my earliest childhood memory. I have a picture in my mind of him swinging me between his legs while I kick a ball against the coal bunker at the rear of our house, before my own legs could be relied upon to get me safely around the back garden. He had his chance to play for Aston Villa and, as we shall see later, there was a bond between us in this respect.

I witnessed his distress and asked, 'What's wrong?' but I was fobbed off with meaningless answers accompanied by the standard response *they* gave in times of distress: 'Why don't you go out to play!' The distress continued for a day or two, or so it seemed. I was not privy to the whispered conversation. It was only when it became clear that there was hope rising out of the ashes of disaster that I was taken aside and told the cause of the disorder that had briefly impinged on our lives. A plane had crashed in Munich in Germany (wherever that was) when it had stopped to refuel on the journey back from Belgrade in Yugoslavia. A close friend of Uncle Bobby's had been on board – Harry Gregg, a Northern Ireland international goalkeeper who played with Manchester United football club. This was a disaster on a large scale. There were many deaths and for a time no one could be certain if Harry Gregg had survived. Thankfully he did and Uncle Bobby's demeanour improved. My parents smiled again and instead of being ordered out to play we were back to the normal: 'Christopher, this is the last time I'll call you in before I get your dad!'

Charlton skips past Blanchflower on the left... he crosses... Brown comes for the ball but just before it reaches his hands in comes Viollet... and it's 8–6 to United in front of a packed Old Trafford...

In our world you played for both teams, and whilst beating imaginary opponents with consummate ease, you would also be taking your turn at doing the Kenneth Wolstenholme commentary. This was the original *Fantasy*

Football League. This was Ballymoney, County Antrim from 1958 to 1962, when I left, never to live there again. My house was in Windsor Gardens, a cul-de-sac, a bird's-eye view of which would give the impression of a Yale key. The round bit at the top of the cul-de-sac was our adventure playground – a place which could be Wimbledon during the tennis championships, the Oval for a test match (although to be truthful there was little interest in cricket), Old Trafford, Wembley or the New York Yankees stadium, depending on the season and the game we decided to play.

Mostly it was football, unless the girls wanted to join in, and then we would reluctantly agree to rounders! At the time it seemed a large area which dwarfed us kids but I've been back a couple of times as a grown-up and it really is disappointingly small. On the three closed sides of the cul-de-sac there were six semi-detached houses in three blocks of two. Each had its own fence and hedge but the best hedge belonged to the Coulter family. It was the perfect shape and size for a goal, at least for kids standing just a few feet tall. Its greatest advantage was that it did not have a house behind it! The Freemans had a great footballing hedge which we used when we had large enough numbers to make two four- or five-a-side teams. The trouble was that you could scorch the crossbar (the top of the hedge) with a twenty-yard volley and the result could be (and often was) a broken window in the Freemans' front room. Then you'd see Dad standing there a day or two later, putty in one hand while the other held the new glass in place. I remember George Coulter once nearly hitting my da with a brilliant shot as he was busy replacing the glass I'd broken earlier with a penalty against Leicester City.

We'd congregate in the cul-de-sac to pick teams. If we had enough players for a game, off we went, but if there were only three or four of us we would play out imaginary games, with one taking on the goalkeeper's role and the others playing 'shooty-in' against him. No one wanted to be the goalkeeper. 'Bags not goalie!' You had to get that in quick. There was no problem when John Michael was there – he liked doing goalkeeper, or at least we believed he did. This would leave me, George and his brother Trevor, and John's brother Kenneth to shoot-in at him. I liked to play on the left side and cross high balls for the others to try to head past John. I also liked to be the commentator. Easy to criticise the others when they fucked up their moves, while conveniently overlooking my own blunders. Mostly we liked to take massive shots from thirty yards, or even three feet, even though we'd promised John there would be no shots from less than ten yards. We loved to send the ball at about eighty miles an hour thumping into the hedge, the impact sending leaves flying in every direction. Branches even fell off on occasion. In our minds, of course, it was not the hedge that stopped the ball, it was the net at some big stadium – Old Trafford or a cup final at Wembley. Windsor Gardens, Ballymoney, was my first Theatre of Dreams.

Byrne to Edwards who sends a superb thirty-yard pass out on to the left wing for Charlton ... he controls it beautifully ... pushes it forward and

unleashes a brilliant shot from outside the box...
top corner... what a goal!

Yes, I favoured Charlton. He wore No 11 on his shirt, and from that day to this, I've had an affinity with left-wingers. Charlton was just a kid then but he was about to become one of the most feared and respected players in world football. He survived the dreadful crash; twenty-three others lost their lives, including eight of the players who had become the most exciting side in English football, and perhaps in Europe.

Later, when I devoured every word I could find about Manchester United, I learned that manager Sir Matt Busby had taken United into Europe the previous season against the advice of the Football Association, which believed that the nation that gave us football was still the premier footballing nation in the world and had nothing to prove in Europe. As a Scotsman, Matt saw through these insular attitudes. He wanted a team that could compete with the best, and at the time Real Madrid were the best in Europe – Puskas, di Stefano, Gento – and we had lost to them in the semi-final in our first appearance in the competition. If Munich hadn't happened we might have been facing them again, this time in the final. They won the European Cup five times in succession, in the first five years of the competition. Europe was important to Matt Busby then, just as it is important to Alex Ferguson and to me now. As I write this the portable television is tuned to UTV for tonight's big game in the European Champions Cup. United are in Austria to play Rapid Vienna, and they must win this game to qualify for the quarter-finals in style.

Peter Schmeichel has just produced a Gordon Banks World Cup 1970-type save to keep the scores level! He's brilliant! Best goalie we've had since Gregg! Oh God, not another of those torturous nights on the nerves, please!

My childhood years in Windsor Gardens were dominated by football, and post-Munich there was only one result I listened for every Saturday night. But I can't claim it was my only interest as we entered the 1960s. I liked pop music, although there was not much to choose from at the time. Cliff Richard and Elvis were big rivals. I favoured Elvis, that is until the Beatles arrived on the scene. We set up a kind of music club which used to meet in our front room every Saturday morning. We had coffee and my ma's lovely sticky buns.

My other preoccupation was the beautiful Jane who lived across the street. Our bedrooms were 'connected' by the telephone line which went from a junction box outside my room to a similar attachment at hers. To make contact we would twang the telephone line and hang out the windows to chat across the darkened street.

Solskjaer just missed an open goal – from three yards out he put it wide. But we are playing much better football now and Rapid Vienna are on the rack. YESSSSSSS! Twenty-fourth minute – Giggs on a run, skips past two defenders, slips the ball to King Eric and he threads one through their last line perfectly into the path of the oncoming Giggsy and he has just put the ball in the net. Man United's

value on the stock market will no doubt soar again
if we hang on to win this one!

What was difficult to comprehend was my desire to
spend time alone with Jane. When I got her alone I was
not sure what I was supposed to do. When you spend
your life playing football in the street, there's little time
to discuss the birds and the bees, let alone interpret
your first sexual stirrings. What was going on? Who do
you ask? What do you say? It was not a problem to
share with your mates.

Solskjaer has just brilliantly turned a defender and
cracked in a superb shot on goal, turned around for
a corner by the Rapid keeper. And as half-time
approaches we get a flash of action from Turin. I'm
praying it's not a goal for the Turks – but no, it's
perfect, a goal for Juventus. We are on our way!

One night I managed to get Jane up to my bedroom, just
the two of us, to talk about homework! Well, how would *you*
have got her attention? We were lying on my bed, the smell
of her perfume exciting my nostrils, chatting aimlessly about
things like English and the enormous bible my parents had.
I fetched the heavy tome, which was about two feet wide
by two-and-a-half feet long and five inches thick, and which
was opened and closed by a brass buckle. I threw it on the
bed and as Jane adjusted position I caught a brief glimpse
of her stockings and suspenders and the flesh at the top of
her thighs. It was all over in a fraction of a second, but what
an effect it had on me! It certainly explained the little button

bumps I'd noticed on her thighs inside the fashionable tight trousers she wore on Saturdays at the music club.

The second half has just begun in Vienna and Giggsy missed from about six yards, an open goal! That could have been it. Goodnight Vienna!

Just a glimpse! For the next two years I kept trying to get another look. I never did. I don't remember ever kissing Jane.

Eventually I took to sending her long letters expressing my deep, undying love for her, but nothing of the kind to worry the prudish British censors who banned *Lady Chatterley's Lover*. I may have got one or two such letters in reply, but when they dried up I remained as dedicated and prolific as ever. Letters rained in on Jane, transported by one of our brothers or sisters. What eventually killed my ardour was the discovery from my mother of all people that Jane had a habit of setting up the ironing board when guests called at her house, to press my love letters into a warm, neat and perfectly flat collection. There you have it lads. Women! Can't trust them.

Sixty-five minutes gone and Solskjaer is off down the right wing, beats the left back and places a cross on to Eric the King's head, but his powerful header fails to bulge the net. Instead it hits the effin' post. He's just having one of those lean spells; seems to be a yard slower in his thinking, if you know what I mean.

From February 1958 I had a new love in my life, one which had greater staying power than Jane and which has given me many more exciting moments. Up until Munich I had enjoyed playing football but had not really become attached to any particular club. Of course I knew of Manchester United – they were, after all, the most success-ful team in England at the time – but it was as if on that tragic day someone drained away all my blood, some sort of Red Devil who appeared secretly in my bedroom at night and replaced my red corpuscles with red, white and black ones. Suddenly my schoolbooks were adorned with the names of United players, living and dead: Geoff Bent, Bobby Charlton, Dennis Viollet, Roger Byrne, Eddie Colman, Duncan Edwards, Mark Jones, David Pegg, Tommy Taylor and Liam Whelan. My efforts did not go unnoticed. One of my primary school teachers snitched on me, writing on my school report that if I dedicated myself to my work as much as I did to decorating my books and schoolbag with the names of Manchester United players, my results would improve dramatically. Thanks! ShemusthavebeenaScouser!

FC Porto, here we come! Le Dieu has just slammed in a second goal in Vienna. Now we're doing a Viennese waltz. The United fans in Austria have been noisy all night and are now singing 'Down by the Riverside', a reference to our clinching last year's FA Carling Premiership title at Middles-borough's Riverside Stadium. Yes, we are in the quarter-finals of this season's European Champions Cup and by the way, in spite of a bad run of defeats,

we are still just half a dozen or so points behind the
league leaders. We've been beaten only three times in
the league. Time enough in May to worry about that.

Munich was a tragedy for other families – those of the
eight journalists who died and the four United officials
who perished. Less than twenty-four hours earlier, nine
reporters did their job, filing reports of the marvellous
3–3 draw with Red Star Belgrade, which was enough to
get United through to the next round 5–4 on aggregate.
Now eight were dead: Alf Clarke, *Manchester Evening
Chronicle*; Tom Jackson, *Manchester Evening News*; Don
Davis, 'Old International' of the *Manchester Guardian*;
George Follows, *Daily Herald*; Archie Ledbrook, *Daily
Mirror*; Eric Thompson, *Daily Mail*; Henry Rose, *Daily
Express*; and former Manchester City goalkeeper Frank
Swift, *News of the World*. First team trainer Tom Curry and
coach Bert Whalley also died, along with club secretary
Walter Crickmer. (He was replaced by the man who
became my penpal, Les Olive.) The death of club director
George Whittaker created an opening for the Edwards
family to begin their long association with United. On 7
February 1958 Louis Edwards was elected to the board, the
support of Matt Busby a crucial element in his election.

Of course I followed the FA Cup run that year, beginning thirteen nights after the air crash with a fifth-round
tie at Old Trafford against Sheffield Wednesday. No one
knew who was going to play, so there was a blank space
in the programme where the United players' names would
normally appear. We got to the final that year but lost
out 2–0 to Bolton Wanderers, although Nat Lofthouse's

second goal should never have been allowed: he bundled Harry Gregg (who was holding the ball) over the line. Lofthouse himself said later, as quoted in *The Hamlyn Illustrated History of Manchester United 1878–1994*: 'I am quite convinced that I did foul Gregg, but you could hardly expect me to argue when the referee gave a goal.' Harry Gregg was reported to be very angry, but in the years ahead he got revenge on Bolton and Lofthouse many times over! After the euphoria of actually getting to Wembley, defeat had a bitter taste but one I was to become accustomed to over the years.

There is no doubt that the air disaster gave United a large sympathetic following throughout Britain and beyond, but in my childhood world I was unaware of the great feeling of jealousy this aroused in other clubs, and which in later years manifested itself in sarcastic comments about United's achievements immediately after Munich.

At primary school we played football at every opportunity and some of my team-mates were destined to become professional players in England, a few even winning international caps. We shared our school playground with the local technical college and it was here that I played football with much older boys – those who became professionals. There was Dessie Dickson, a prolific goal-scorer with Coleraine, who got to play for Northern Ireland four times. But it was Shaun Dunlop who was my role model – he was forever combing his hair, which made him look just like Ed Byrne as 'Kookie' in the television show *77 Sunset Strip*. He could do all sorts of tricks with the ball – and we played with a tennis ball. What control!

What a shot! What speed! His skills took him to Arsenal as a youth and he represented Northern Ireland at Wembley in the 1963 final of the 16th International Youth Championship, the mini World Cup. England won 4–0 and would have scored more but for a dazzling display of goal-keeping by the 'certain-to-be-world-class' Pat Jennings.

Things may not have worked out as well for Shaun in England as they did for his team-mate Jennings, but his return home to star in Irish League football with Coleraine proved to be a bonus for spectators. He was the perfect partner for his old school friend Dessie Dickson. Dunlop was a prolific enough scoring winger, but with Dickson in the centre-forward role, he became the provider. It was at this time that Dickson won the European Golden Boot award for scoring over sixty goals in one season. According to *News Letter* football correspondent Billy Oliver, Dessie was asked at the presentation of the award if he could explain his goal-scoring prowess. He baffled the Europeans with his answer that 'Shaun goes doon the wing and crosses them o'er and I just nod them in.' Another player to feature in that highly successful Coleraine side of the 1970s was someone of my own age, Liam Beckett.

As I played football with these talented mates and prepared for a lifetime in United's cause I was totally unaware of events going on around me, such as the IRA's border campaign which had begun in 1956 and continued until 1962. I had no interest in religion or politics. So as the 1960s began, my life started to focus more and more on Manchester United. I was still blissfully ignorant of the great changes which were about to befall our family.

2

ON THE MOVE

A nomad. That's what I was for a year or so. Moving from school to school, home to home. As Manchester United set about rekindling their team from the ashes of the Munich air disaster, I was facing significant changes in my world. For a start there was a confrontation with failure. In 1961 I was a victim of the eleven-plus blues, although my parents assured me it was due to nervousness on the day, not to lack of ability. It appears they checked up on my marks and were satisfied that I had sufficient ability to go to a grammar school. This meant paying school fees for that first year, in the hope that I would pass the 'review' to qualify for the scholarship denied me by my failure. Thankfully, in this respect I did not let them down.

In Ballymoney, grammar school meant Dalriada – one of those institutions that survive, indeed thrive, on tradition. My first day there was a culture shock, especially when I learned that it was a rugby-playing school that looked down on football, or 'soccer' as they insisted on calling it. The realisation that there would be no football, only rugby, was devastating enough on my first day – but worse, it seemed no one here was interested in my team's progress since Munich. Bringing Manchester United into the hallowed, marble-floored corridors of Dalriada was like trying to sell rosary beads to Ian Paisley.

My new classmates came from much further afield

than Ballymoney. Consequently, many were unknown to me. While some of my old playmates from primary school were busy preparing themselves for professional football, I was contemplating rugby – a game I viewed with deep suspicion. For a start the ball was an odd shape and the players did not know how to caress it properly with the foot to make it do what they wanted it to do. Worst of all, they picked the bloody thing up and ran with it. It was like playing with fifteen goalkeepers. Very strange indeed. Once I began to play the game, I discovered why they were so inept at kicking it. They played with steel toecaps in their boots! How could you possibly persuade the ball to do your bidding? Accurate kicking was clearly not a priority. Mind you, kickers have since become much more important to rugby and they now have some who – properly equipped in the boot department – have a fine 'feel' for the ball. Once I was involved in the action, rugby did offer some pleasure. Being a 'short-arse' with a low centre of gravity, I was drawn towards the scrum-half position. Scrum-halves are constantly at the centre of the action and that suited me fine.

Football remained my passion, however, and when someone (almost certainly Uncle Bobby) gave me a rugby ball as a Christmas present that year, I viewed it as an act of betrayal. What bloody use was a rugby ball? The very shape precluded any accurate prediction of what it might do next when kicked up the garden, bouncing innocently towards the hedge one moment, menacingly towards our neighbour's greenhouse the next. You could not dribble the ball up and down the garden like a football. Believe me, I tried. Nor kick it against a wall with both feet to improve your control. To make use of the rugby ball you needed others to join in. With a football, all you needed was a bit of imagination and you could spend hours on your own scoring winning goals in cup finals or in vital games to clinch the league title. Once away from school, it was back to street football, our own Theatre of Dreams, and following the fortunes of my team.

Like me, United made an indifferent start to the decade immediately post-Munich, until that wonderful cup final victory over Leicester in 1963. In the 1958–59 season the team had played with the tremendous tail wind of sympathetic support brought about by the plane disaster, managing to finish second in the league, scoring a hundred goals and watching home attendance figures reach record levels. It became a regular occurrence for more than 60,000 to pack into Old Trafford. The club bought Albert Quixall from Sheffield Wednesday for £45,000, a British record fee at the time. From what I could determine from newspaper reports, he could dazzle in one game and disappear in the next. He managed just four goals in thirty-three appearances. Bobby Charlton and Dennis Viollet were our top scorers – Charlton scoring twenty-nine from thirty-eight games and Viollet twenty-one from thirty-seven. The really good news was that Harry Gregg was back to his best form, playing in forty-one of the forty-two league games.

The following season, however, we finished a poor seventh in the league and were dumped out of the FA Cup in the fifth round; it was as if the post-Munich honeymoon was over, although we still managed to score ninety-nine goals. The big development at Old Trafford was the construction of a roof for the Stretford End, giving cover to the famous terrace which could accommodate (not always comfortably) 22,000 spectators. This area of the stadium was the heart and soul of the club. It was where I longed to be, my spiritual home at Old Trafford. Even though I had never even set foot in the stadium, I just knew that when I went there it would be to make myself hoarse at the Stretford End.

When Harry Gregg was injured in the 1960–61 season, and with reserve keeper David Gaskell also injured, another young Irishman got his big chance. Ronnie Briggs had been a schoolboy international when he signed as a professional for United at the age of seventeen. Nine months later, in January 1961, he had this wonderful opportunity to impress. He certainly made his mark. His début was in an away match at Leicester where he conceded six goals, then in his next game at Old Trafford in the FA Cup, Sheffield Wednesday put seven past him in a humiliating 7–2 defeat. The only positive aspect of Dalriada was that the humiliation of United went unnoticed by my rugger-playing schoolmates! Remarkably, although Briggs's Manchester United career ended before it had begun (he played only eight more league games for United the following season), he went on to represent Northern Ireland in 1962 as a United player and again in 1965 when he played with Swansea Town.

My commission at Dalriada was as brief as Briggs's career at Old Trafford. After just one year there it was time for a change. My father was taking up a new job with a company in the mid-Ulster area and I was to switch to the Rainey Endowed School in Magherafelt. While my parents searched for a new home I was sent ahead to live in digs so that I could begin with the new school term in September. Again it was a rugby school and our team included a future Ulster and junior Ireland player, Alan 'Raker' McLean. Little of significance marked my short spell at Rainey except perhaps my romance with Rhoda Leacock. This was a difficult courtship for us both, as she travelled by bus from her home in Tobermore. We rarely got time alone together and for the six months I attended Rainey our romance was based entirely on letters. Whole rainforests being destroyed for Rhoda and me to maintain a romance that never even reached the kiss and cuddle stage.

The most embarrassing moment in my life came one morning in the French class, which was not one of Rhoda's classes. The French teacher, an elderly man, was wandering down an aisle towards my desk. I did not see him, just heard his drone in the background as I caught up with the latest love instalment from Rhoda, my eyes fixed under the desk where I held the pages with that distinctive sweet aroma I now associated with Rhoda. I had barely got beyond the first page when suddenly my head jolted forward, not of its own volition. He was standing by my side. 'Class, it would appear that Mr Moore has no need to pay attention,' he said loudly. Seeing the cause of my distraction, he reached down and grabbed the pages before I could hide them. Oh, no! I thought, he's not going to . . . but yes, he did.

Suddenly he had the full attention of everyone in the room. The whole class sat in absolute silence, hanging on every word the old git read out – our undying love for one another laid bare. Mind you, when he reached a sentence in which Rhoda said she loved me so much she would let me lie on top of her, it was his turn to go bright red! Realising that he was trespassing on what should be private feelings, he threw the letter back to me and instructed me to read it in my own time. As we left for our next class, I felt compelled to find out what all this meant. I asked Alfie Suitor what the hell Rhoda was thinking of when she said 'lie on top of me'. That was the day I learned about the birds and the bees, as Alfie excelled himself, ably assisted by a girl in our class, in explaining what I might want to do with my erect penis if given the chance. Alas, I never did get that chance with Rhoda Leacock. I was snatched away before we could consummate our love.

In Magherafelt, as in Ballymoney, circumstances prevented me from putting down roots. My family was on the move again. Not that they had ever actually made it to Magherafelt. There was a complete change of plan. Instead of County Derry we were destined for Scotland, where my da had received a better job offer. Blairgowrie in Perthshire was where I would enrol in my third school inside a year. But before I could celebrate the fact that my new school played football, indeed before I even came within sight of the place, my arrival in the land of Burns and haggis was marked by an inauspicious event which threatened to brand me for life. Within twenty-four hours of reaching Scotland I was arrested.

It happened like this. My parents had already visited our new home-town and purchased a house at Pine Grove, Carsie, two miles or so outside Blairgowrie on the main road to Perth and just opposite the famous Rosemount golf club, of which more later. They had made contact with a local family, the Browns, who had one child, a boy of my age by the name of Ewan. On the Saturday we arrived I met Ewan and we hit it off immediately. After a brief trip on his tandem – my first attempt to ride such a contraption – there followed a tour of the local terrain. Carsie was little more than a cluster of houses around a small piece of rough parkland dominated by gorse bushes. As I soon discovered, this small piece of real estate was to play a vital part in our leisure lives. Ewan pointed out places of likely interest to thirteen-year-olds and introduced a number of the local children, then we took off on our bikes along a bumpy dirt track which led down a steep hill and up to a farm situated on the high ground opposite. The lane leading up to the farm buildings formed a natural causeway between two lakes.

We cycled along the tractor tracks bordering the lake on the left, chatting busily and trying to upstage each other with stories about working on the land. My only experience had been with my Uncle Sammy and was mainly in the area of animal husbandry: looking after pigs. Our agricultural interest was a common bond, and when we came upon a tractor with a silage-cutter still hooked up, we competed to tell stories about how much experience we had of driving tractors. My experience was very limited but I could not admit that. Discovering that the keys of this tractor had been left in the ignition, we were determined to demonstrate our driving skills. We cast aside the bicycles and threw ourselves up on to the tractor. Ewan got there first and soon we were taking turns driving the tractor at full speed around and around the field, in boundless, timeless pleasure. The smell of burning rubber interrupted us; a level on the silage-cutter had been rubbing against a tyre, from which a small pall of smoke rose when the vehicle was at a standstill. Panic! We carefully reversed the smouldering tyre and the silage-cutter itself into the lake bordering one side of the field. Once it had cooled we moved the tractor carefully back to its original position and fled.

For Ewan and myself, farming was the only common interest. Ewan did not like football. He did not play football. He had never heard of Manchester United. Nevertheless I enjoyed his company. We spent the last moments of daylight checking out his rabbit snares! Ewan was a poacher and could sell his rabbits to a butcher in town for between 7/6d and 10/-.

Day one in Scotland ended with an meal in our new kitchen, followed by unpacking boxes in our bedrooms. My brother Geoff and I shared one of the three bedrooms and my sister Melody had a room of her own. It was one of those nights when sleep came easily. Peace settled on our house as all five members of the family drifted off into dreams of our new lives in bonnie Scotland.

At eleven o'clock next morning my dreams became a nightmare. As I struggled down for breakfast I paused at the small landing window that overlooked the street at the front of the house. My attention was attracted by the arrival of a police car. Totally absorbed, I watched as the occupants got their bearings, manoeuvred the car to a halt outside our gate and proceeded up the path towards the house. I felt ill. It was one of those moments when you do not know for sure what is about to happen but a voice inside you is screaming: 'They are here for you!' So indeed it turned out to be. Me in my pyjamas. Humiliation. The sergeant firing questions. That's when I realised that it had to be Ewan who had fitted me up for this. He was the only person I was acquainted with in this part of the planet, and now that I focused on the car from ground level I thought I could make out Ewan's silhouette in the back.

The whole family watched my ordeal open-mouthed. Here I was, an innocent in love, sex and crime, yet this bloody big sergeant was standing waiting for my answers. He asked if I had been driving a tractor in the past twenty-four hours. Either I had been or I had not. But no sound came from my lips. On the basis of books I had read, I had instinctively decided to adopt Al Capone's interview technique – whatever you say, say nothing. The sergeant told my parents he would have to take me to the station. *He thinks he can break me there! No chance, mate.* He waited while I got dressed and escorted me to the car to join, yes, Ewan in the rear seat. Before we got to the station, indeed before we left our estate, the cops told us the farmer (Archie Stewart) did not wish to press charges. He simply wanted the power drive for the silage-cutter back. Would we go to the field and look for it? Sure, mister. Fortunately we found the missing driveshaft (which we must have mislaid during our adventures of the previous day without even being aware of it) and Farmer Stewart was delighted to receive it. In fact he was so pleased to learn of our enthusiasm for farming in general and tractor-driving in particular that he offered both of us jobs.

Over the next few years we got to drive tractors for

real: baling hay, bringing in the corn harvest for storage in enormous silos. Ewan even found love down on the farm. He ended up marrying one of Archie Stewart's daughters! There was still just one love in my life, and that was football – although Ewan and I still managed to cause trouble with our various enterprises. Passengers on the bus taking us to school were less than impressed by our 'screw' trick. This was where we would loosen the screws holding the seats together. We did not remove them, just loosened them. Then we would watch as the combination of the weight of passengers and the normal vibrations of the bus did the rest. Suddenly the seat would collapse, scattering old dears and young executives on to the floor in a most undignified manner. We thought it was hilarious. The bus company, the passengers and the police were less than impressed. The headmaster was not pleased either and as my five years at his school went on he had good reason to be suspicious of me and Ewan Brown.

The Rosemount championship golf course was just across the main Blairgowrie-Perth road at Carsie where we lived. It was a natural playground which held a mystical allure for boys and girls in their early teens. As well as looking for golf balls, playing hide-and-seek, cops and robbers, cowboys and Indians, Ewan and I found another important use for the golf course. This involved me 'borrowing' the brand-new saw from my father's garage, one of those big saws which take two people to use, one at either end. We used the saw to remove trees from the golf course, cutting the branches into logs and taking them round to the houses of old people on our estate. We pulled the logs around on a cart made from old pram wheels and a few planks of wood. The old people were delighted, the golf course manager was outraged and my father was livid when confronted with his saw, which had been found hidden on the course. Sherwood Forest it was not, and our Robin Hood act did not impress. The police were once again called in to investigate but because the manager was a neighbour friendly with my parents, the club decided not to press charges. We got off the hook with a stern warning. My father never got his saw back, though.

At a later stage we had access to the keys to the school and would often make use of them. Our favourite trick was to prepare the school for the new intake of pupils from primary school. The night before their arrival we would enter the school, keeping a close eye out for the 'janny' (janitor) who lived in a bungalow at the school gates, and, armed with screwdrivers, we would change the signs around on internal doors. For example, the head-master's sign would be exchanged with the sign for the boys' toilet, the girls' toilet would become the French class, the science classroom would become the gym-nasium or the history classroom, and so on.

My friend and next-door neighbour, Dave Robb, along with Dave Rodgers and a couple of others, used the keys to demonstrate their grasp of the sciences. They made a smoke bomb which they intended to explode in the assembly hall during morning assembly. Wires from under the stage were brought to the back of the hall where we all stood so that one of the lads could detonate the device using one of the metal heels attached to his shoe. How-ever, Dave Robb was spotted trying to manoeuvre his foot on to the wires during prayers. Three of the gang were expelled but later permitted to return after a plea from the Physics teacher, Mr Stuart Moore (no relation), who was so impressed by their misdirected abilities that he detonated the device on the school playing fields in front of the entire class. There were to be other adventures at Blairgowrie High School.

In 1963, 100,000 people watched the game in Wembley stadium in which United won the FA Cup, beating Leicester City 3-1. This victory in the biggest television event of the English football year was a glittering occasion for me, especially because relegation to Division Two had seemed more than possible in a season which marked yet another transition. As happens in every football club, one team was fading gradually, as injury, old age and transfers broke up what had been a unified entity. Then, as that squad disintegrated, another entity began to form itself into a sparkling, attacking and cohesive unit. This was when Matt Busby saw the birth of the team that would rival the achievements of his pre-Munich Babes. It was the beginning of the Law, Charlton and Best dynasty. Of course Best did not appear in the 1963 cup final side, which began the game as the underdogs against a Leicester team which had finished fourth in the league and was making its second cup final appearance in three years. They had Gordon Banks but we had Denis Law. Winning the cup in 1963 was the biggest boost for United since league successes in 1956 and 1957.

Our team that day was: Gaskell; Dunne, Cantwell; Crerand, Foulkes, Setters; Giles, Quixall, Herd, Law, Charlton. My leaping five feet in the air might have been sufficient to secure gold in the junior Olympics, but it did not impress my parents as the landing area was contaminated with china cups and saucers filled with tea. But who cared. Law had just danced his way into a scoring position, magnificently beating Banks to hit home our first goal. He had come to us for a record transfer fee of £115,000 from the Italian side Torino, one of only two signings made that season by Sir Matt. The other involved a Scotsman as well; the purchase of Pat Crerand for £56,000 was yet another masterpiece of jigsaw building by the great man. Crerand's skills were sublime – he could dissect a defence with a fifty-yard pass – and yet he could be the hard man when the going got tough. Like Law he had the impetuous Celtic temperament. But he showed incredible commitment. Winning at Wembley in 1963 with these two new signings augured well for the future, and the best was yet to come.

We sold seven players that year, three of them Irishmen. Two were from north of the border – Northern Ireland internationals Sammy McMillan and Jimmy Nicholson were sold for £8,000 each to Wrexham and Huddersfield respectively. The third was a Dubliner, thereafter known as 'the one who got away'. Johnny Giles played in the cup final but he and Busby did not see eye to eye so he was sold to Leeds for £37,500 – a bargain. He was to taunt us and haunt us for years, scoring over 100 goals for the Yorkshire side. He became a world-class player in a team which grew arrogant because of its domination of the English game for so much of the 1970s, although 0-0 or 1-0 were regularly the scores in Leeds games. While Leeds gave their public efficiency rather than flamboyance, we proved that winning did not mean sacrificing entertainment.

3

FLOWER OF SCOTLAND

Frank Matthews sat on the sofa, trying to divide his eye contact between my mother in the chair on his right and my father in the chair on his left. It was painful to witness. Billy and Kathleen were not for budging. Me? All my pleas fell on stony-deaf ears.

'Listen,' Frank said with exasperation and desperation creeping into his voice, 'they will look after his education. If he wants to go to university, they'll put him through.'

That clinched the argument for me. I was not prepared for this development. Frank had neglected to mention it when he gave me advance warning of his call to see my folks. Lord, I thought, they didn't see the swerve Frank put on the ball. This was a goal. But Billy and Kathleen still said no.

'He has to concentrate on his O-Levels,' said my mother. The exams were coming up in the next few months and I was expected to spend more and more time alone in my bedroom with schoolbooks. In the early weeks of 1967, the impact of my parents' refusal to budge on a point of principle – their principle – was enormous, although it was to be some years before I truly and fully understood the depth of my disappointment. Not coming to terms with it much sooner proved to be my downfall.

Frank Matthews was the father of a school chum and, as it happened, a fellow-worker in a local bakery and grocer's store, P. J. Robertson's, where I had a part-time job as a messenger boy delivering groceries on one of those bicycles with a big basket sitting over the front wheel. He was also a football scout, although I did not know this when I started calling at Neil's house almost as soon as I started school in Blairgowrie in 1963. As a baker Frank worked during the night so he was often around on those afternoons when Neil and I kicked a ball about in their garden. At first there was no indication that Frank's interest in my football was anything other than that of a friend's father.

My memory is that the Matthews' garden had a small orchard in one half and a large grassy area in the other. It was enclosed on three sides by hedges and mature trees and had an enormous gable wall on the fourth side, a perfect place to improve skills. We spent hours bashing the ball against that wall in what was a bit like adapted squash. We had to alternate our shots between left and right feet, thereby polishing the touch of the 'good' foot and strengthening the performance of the weaker one. Frank spent time telling us how to improve our skills. A man of medium height, he had one of those old-fashioned hairstyles, a throwback to the sleek Brylcreem look of the 1950s. He walked with a permanent limp, although I don't ever remember hearing how he received this injury. But when he kicked a shot demonstration-style against the gable wall, it was clear that he had a deep knowledge of how to treat a ball.

My own father rarely played football with us. To be blunt, he was crap. The moment the ball arrived at his feet it would fly off randomly in any direction. He wore brogues with hard leather soles which stuck out a quarter of an inch from the stitching to the upper, and boy, could they lift lumps out of your shins if you were unfortunate enough to make contact. Fortunately, the way Billy controlled a ball made it virtually unnecessary to tackle him.

Frank Matthews, meanwhile, was becoming my football mentor, someone who encouraged me to keep practising, stressing the need for commitment. I needed little encouragement to keep me going. The side pockets of my school blazer were stretched out of shape by the tennis balls I took everywhere. We would rush into school half an hour early each morning so we could have a match in the playground. We did the same every breaktime and lunchtime.

After school we went to Lochee park and played two-touch football. You got one touch to trap the ball, and the other was to distribute it to your playing partner or to shoot at goal. This game sharpened the mind, encouraging players to think about where they wanted the ball to be after the first touch. One-two interchanges were crucial to victory. There's no doubt that using a tennis ball improved skill. You noticed it immediately when playing with the full-size ball.

Sharpening our awareness in Lochee park proved surprisingly useful when it came to playing competitive games for the school, but it never totally obliterated the desire in each of us to take the ball past crowds of opposition players and score the greatest goal of all time. Such fanciful efforts were denounced as 'bloody daft' from the touchline by big Jake, the PE teacher, and his sidekick Bill, our geography teacher. These two wanted to stress the 'team' aspect of the game, to persuade us that we must play together and think as one, not as eleven individuals. Funnily enough, they applied the same principles outside the school gates.

Later on when I was eighteen we happened to meet Bill and Jake in the local pub where we were trying out our first pints of beer. We were surprised when they asked us to join them. We sat talking with them for more than an hour about the evils of drink, the risks of drunkenness and the need to appreciate alcohol while remaining aware of its dangerous potential. In short, Bill and Jake wanted us to understand that drink was something to be enjoyed in moderation. To prove their point, they bought us a pint each while we continued the conversation.

After that they would occasionally bring the team out for a drink, but this cosy occasional arrangement ended when we got pissed one Saturday before an important cup game away to Harris High School in Dundee. The trouble was that Denis Jakobs, a close friend of mine, brought along a large bottle of Scotch. Denis looked after the drinks cellar at the home of a retired British Army colonel (Colonel Brodie) where he lived with his mother, who kept house for the colonel. At the rear of the bus on the way from Blairgowrie to Dundee the bottle of Scotch was being passed around surreptitiously, players ducking down behind the seats to imbibe. We made it on to the pitch without being found out. But then things went wrong. One of our players set off on a marvellous solo run down the wing, finishing his run with a rasping drive from the edge of the penalty area which left the goalkeeper diving at thin air as the ball whizzed past him into the net at about eighty miles an hour. The tragedy was that the player concerned had scored one of the most spectacular own goals ever witnessed. Bill and Jake were understandably devastated. The headmaster ordered an enquiry, but that was when we decided to show tremendous team spirit, collectively remaining silent under intense questioning. We were reinstated as a team a few weeks later and there was never a repeat of such stupidity.

Of course, practice continued every day. Football dominated everything. Even on my own, I would be out under the streetlights playing my fantasy games – dribbling past imaginary opponents, crashing home thirty-yard drives from twelve yards out. While I was living out my fantasies in the school yard and in the streets around the house, United were emerging as a real force in the English game, playing an exciting brand of attacking football. The FA Cup final victory over Leicester in 1963 was the start of this rebuilding process, but perhaps the most significant date came four months later. The game on Saturday 14 September was a home fixture at Old Trafford, and we beat West Bromwich Albion 1–0. The headline in that day's *Manchester Evening News* highlighted the real relevance of what was otherwise a routine Division One fixture: 'Boy Best Flashes in Red Attack'. At seventeen years of age, George Best had made his first appearance for the United senior team.

Best was a true genius with the ball. His outstanding skills in dribbling around defenders, three or four of them at once on occasion, made him without doubt the best and most exciting player in the world. The arguments on this subject have raged on and on over the years. Ian St John and Jimmy Greaves once participated in a television programme which took the form of a jury sitting in judgement on great footballers. One of those programmes put George Best (who had long since retired from top-class football) up against Kevin Keegan. Jimmy Greaves had by then already described Best as the 'greatest footballer of my lifetime' and must have been as baffled as his audience when the voting favoured Keegan over Best. Admittedly, Keegan was a special player, who absolutely dedicated to making himself fitter and improving every aspect of his game. He deserved every success he achieved as a player for Liverpool, Newcastle, Hamburg and Southampton. But George Best had much more. He had wonderful natural skills. He had balance, tremendous shooting ability, mesmerising dribbling skills, and a wicked sense of humour which expressed itself in some of his showman tactics such as sitting on the ball during the game, as if to allow his tortured opponents time to recover and regroup. He was also tenacious in the tackle. Even Pele and Eusebio could not match him. Even though his career did not last as long as that of some others, for the short time he graced top class football he was for me the best the world has ever seen.

In that first season George Best made a total of seventeen league appearances, scoring four goals. United finished runners-up in Division One and had a strange European campaign in the Cup Winners' Cup. In the first round they devoured the Dutch side Willem II of Tilburg 7-2 on aggregate. Then they beat the holders Tottenham Hotspur in the next round. Spurs had beaten us 2-0 in the first leg at White Hart Lane. In the early 1960s Spurs were our *bête noire*, beginning the decade by making history with the first Double since Aston Villa's in 1897. I sat down at about 10.30 pm that evening to watch recorded highlights of the game on television to find out if we could overturn the mighty Spurs.

It was a terrific game, marred only by the broken leg Spurs player Dave Mackay suffered in the first ten minutes. We won 4-1 and confidently approached the quarter-finals against Portuguese side, Sporting Lisbon. The first leg at Old Trafford witnessed a poor United performance but as I saw for myself on television, we managed to win 4-1 with a Denis Law hat-trick, two from penalties. Two weeks later as our place in the draw for the semi-finals seemed assured, I listened on radio as United were stuffed 5-0 in the return leg in Lisbon. Five nil! We were out of the European Cup Winners' Cup. What a shambles. A few days before this debacle, we had lost in the semi-final of the FA Cup to West Ham (3-1). Matt Busby was appalled by United's most humiliating perform-ance ever in Europe. Although we resumed our winning ways in the league, our season was effectively over – killed off in just a few days in the spring of 1964.

As United's season died ignominiously, my football career was blossoming and my interest in the pop charts was increasingly focusing on the Rolling Stones. When I discovered that they were playing a concert in Leeds in July 1964 and that the school Army Cadet Force was having a two-week summer camp in that city at that time, I enlisted! For just a few pounds there was subsidised transport to Leeds, free accommodation and – as it happened – a chance to meet Lulu (the support act) and

Mick Jagger himself. Mind you, my experience of authoritarian 'army' life was an eye-opener, which ensured that I resigned my 'commission' immediately upon our return.

Matt Busby spent his summer making crucial decisions about how we could go one better than runners-up in the League Championship. He turned to Ireland to make one of the two key signings which finally secured our first championship-winning team for eight years. Goalkeeper Pat Dunne was signed from Shamrock Rovers for just £10,500 – making thirty-seven league appearances out of a possible forty-two. The other signing was that of goal-scoring winger John Connolly from Burnley for £60,000. He managed fifteen goals in forty-two outings. The 1964–65 season put the smile back on Matt Busby's face as we stormed through an entire league campaign with a team playing brilliant attacking football, conceding only thirteen goals at Old Trafford as the Best-Law-Charlton partnership really began to bite the opposition. In this glorious championship-winning season, Best appeared in forty-one games, with ten goals, Bobby Charlton in forty-one games with ten goals and Denis Law had thirty-six games with twenty-eight goals. David Herd supported this illustrious trio by contributing twenty goals in thirty-seven games. Leeds beat us in a replayed FA Cup semi-final and finished runners-up to us in the league.

What was frustrating for me about all this success at Old Trafford was that Manchester was a few hundred miles away and I had no opportunity to see the team play. As my own football career began to lift off I still found time to write copiously to United's secretary Les Olive – asking for match tickets (always to no avail because of the club's token scheme, aimed, quite rightly, at giving regular attenders first choice), or seeking (always unsuccessfully) a discarded player's shirt, or even once offering my services to arrange a pre-season friendly with Dundee at their Dens Park ground.

I had stood on the terracing at Dens Park with my father watching Scottish First Division games but my greatest moment at Dens Park was the day I turned up for a trial game. Running out on to the pitch from the dressing rooms was a big thrill, even though the terraces were unoccupied; my imagination did the rest. I managed to crack home not one, but two twenty-yard specials against Dundee's goalkeeper. The result was an invitation to train with the club twice a week. From the outset at Dundee they determined that I needed to build up my strength and I was put on a special diet – two raw eggs every morning before school, mixed with a little milk and glucose to make it more palatable, and the same again at bedtime. It was a small club which in the 1960–61 season had stunned Scottish football by winning the League Championship. Some of those medal-winning players had moved on by the time I arrived for my brief spell at Dens Park – the likes of Alan Gilzean (to Spurs) and Ian Ure (to Arsenal). But Scottish fullback Alex Hamilton was still there.

I watched in awe as these international players messed about during and after training. It was all a bit much for me as a fifteen-year-old, there at Dundee training and playing on a pitch where so many famous players had strutted their stuff. There was a young lad at Dundee called Charles Stuart who took me aside and suggested that I would fare better if I got a chance in England. He had contacts at Chelsea (where he had been for a time, I believe) so he offered to write to Chelsea manager Tommy Docherty on my behalf. However, the Doc responded in writing to say he had an abundance of young players in the system at Stamford Bridge so he could not offer me any future there. My future at Dundee was looking no better because they told me I needed more competitive games than they could offer. Someone at Dundee said they wanted me to go to Arbroath to join their boys' club in order to build up experience. Dundee would keep an eye on me for the future.

Getting to and from Dundee for training had been relatively easy – there was a good bus service – although I had to go straight from school on training nights. I was more dependent on my father when I moved to Arbroath – it was further north than Dundee and impossible to get to from Blairgowrie by public transport of any kind. At the time Arbroath were in the Scottish Second Division and had the longest serving manager in British football, Albert Henderson. To me he was a wonderful man, a gentle soul who made a fuss over my arrival and who was a tremendous motivator. We juniors trained with the first team and the club paid my father travelling expenses for bringing me to Gayfield (their home ground) twice a week for training. Mind you, there were occasions in the height of winter when we simply could not make the journey through the snowstorms on the hills between Blairgowrie and Dundee. But Mr Henderson was very forgiving and on the few occasions I missed training, he still considered me for the reserve team, or at least the boys' club which was used as a reserve team. My closest friend at Arbroath was Tom Cargill, a local player who spent the remainder of his career there.

During my time with Arbroath in 1966, England won the World Cup and Manchester United had their greatest achievement of the decade. In the European Cup campaign we reached the quarter-finals, facing the might of Portugal's Benfica. The first leg was at Old Trafford before a crowd of 64,000. United, inspired by Bobby Charlton, played the only way they knew how, and from the outset peppered the Benfica goal. Benfica, with the wonderfull silky skills of Eusebio, would be no pushovers; they had won the European Cup twice and had twice been losing finalists. First blood was drawn by the visitors on a counter-attack, a Eusebio cross headed home by Augusto. By half-time we were ahead 2–1 with goals from Herd and Law. Fifteen minutes into the second half Noel Cantwell headed one home to make it 3–1, but Benfica managed a second goal before full time. Living up to a 3–2 lead in the second leg at Benfica's Stadium of Light, where they had never suffered a defeat in nineteen European matches, was considered an impossible challenge – especially when United supporters recalled our humiliating 5–0 defeat at the hands of Sporting Lisbon two years earlier. The date of the second-leg game was 9 March 1966. It is a day that will live long in the memory of all United supporters.

At school that day, there was much merriment and sarcasm directed at yours truly as I noisily proclaimed that United would stuff Benfica. Inside, I was full of doubts, but to reveal them would be an act of treason. Indeed, even harbouring such feelings was extremely uncomfortable, as if you were stabbing your own team in the back.

There was to be no live television coverage of this momentous occasion; radio commentary would have to do. Football in Lochee park was played in frantic fashion after school that day, nervous tension making me risk wild, reckless tackles and lose concentration on the ball. Les Sim's team enjoyed a rare victory over us and I set off for home and the family meal in a frustrated state. If only I could get out there, in front of 90,000 frantic Portuguese fans, I knew I could help the team to win this one. But I was stuck here in Scotland, my only challenge the evening's fantasy game in the street outside.

Finally it was bedtime, the moment of truth as I listened on the transistor under the covers. My younger brother lay asleep in his bed opposite. But not for long. Before play began, Eusebio received the European Footballer of the Year award. Twelve minutes into the game it was clear that the wrong player had presented himself for the honour. Best had scored two goals and had a third disallowed. I responded by leaping out of bed, crash-landing on the floor and stretching out a hand to waken Geoff so we could share the moment. By the fifteenth minute we were 3-0 ahead thanks to a strike by John Connolly. Shay Brennan scored an own goal which gave the Benfica fans their only cheer of the night, before Bobby Charlton and Pat Crerand completed our 5-1 stuffing of the Portuguese champions. It was the next evening before I got to see the goals on television. What a night! And there in the thick of the action was Uncle Bobby's good friend Harry Gregg. Our team that memorable night was: Gregg; Brennan, Dunne; Crerand, Foulkes, Stiles; Best, Law, Charlton, Herd, Connolly. Eleven international players – four English, three Scots, two Northern Ireland and two Republic of Ireland.

Best arrived back in England dressed in a long black leather coat and a sombrero. The newspapers gave him the name 'El Beatle', because his rugged good looks and his long hair, at Beatle length, made him look more like a pop star than a footballer. This was the beginning of a new era for professional football in general and for Best in particular. (Though some might argue that it was the beginning of the end of George Best's footballing career, as a whole new world of business opportunity and image exploitation swallowed up the nineteen-year-old.)

Few could deny that our performance in Lisbon was the finest exhibition of attacking football since the heyday of Real Madrid. The Spanish club had dominated the European Cup since the beginning of the competition in the 1955–56 season, winning it five times in succession. I had watched Real Madrid on television in the 1960 final at Hampden Park in Glasgow against Eintracht Frankfurt, winning 7–3 in spectacular fashion in front of 127,621 spectators. It was a memorable game, with the greatest strike force in the history of European football scoring the goals – three to di Stefano and four to Puskas. But it was not just the great football which gave me cause to remember that moment as a ten-year-old, because as I viewed the event on television, I bent over to pick up my pyjamas and the door of the Rayburn behind me gave my bottom third degree burns. For weeks afterwards I suffered the indignity of having the dressings changed daily at home by Nurse Ena Byrnes.

That was then, this was now. This was the year we should have been the first British team to lift the European Cup, but we were beaten to the honour by Glasgow Celtic. In 1967 they took on Inter Milan in the final in Lisbon, winning 2-1. I celebrated that victory with school friend and Celtic fanatic Denis Jakobs, and how he delighted in the fact that his club had beaten mine to the title of European Champions.

About the time Celtic were winning the European Cup, Manchester United were busy winning the League Championship again, clinching the title with a resounding 6-1 away win against the 1966 World Cup winners. Confused? Let me clarify. The 6-1 stuffing was meted out to West Ham United, a team which that day included three of England's World Cup winning team – Bobby Moore, Martin Peters and Geoff Hurst. West Ham supporters claimed theirs was the only club side to win the World Cup, given that Peters and Hurst had scored all the goals in the final against West Germany. UTV presenter Mike Nesbitt often repeats this as some form of mantra. Personally, I think he and all the other West Ham supporters have gone as soft as the bubbles they are so fond of blowing down at Upton Park.

England's World Cup victory received a mixed response in Scotland. Perhaps the best illustration of the feelings of the nation is the fact that as the final was played out at Wembley Stadium, Denis Law was having a game of golf at his local course near Manchester. He is said to have been 'devastated' when news was brought to him of England's success. I watched the final in the staff restroom at Smedley's factory in Blairgowrie, where I had a summer job processing peas. Sometimes to break the monotony, we would swap the as yet unfilled pea cans and strawberry cans from one production line to the other, then put them back in the proper lines. It appealed to my juvenile sense of humour to think of some poor soul looking forward to strawberries and ice cream and finding peas in his strawberry can!

These were the days of flower power, long hair, bell-bottoms, pill popping, alcohol and promiscuity. My wages – and at £30 a week tax-free during the school holidays they were quite formidable for the mid-1960s – meant I could buy luxuries like albums and clothes, essentials like drinks for girlfriends, and in later years petrol to run my father's car. My album collection was made up mostly of the Beatles, Bob Dylan, the Stones and Jimi Hendrix. The clothes were wild and loud. Op-art shirts in black-and-white, purples and greens. A green frock-coat was a gas, but my mother detested it (and virtually every other item of clothing I chose for myself). I took to hiding it in the woods near the house (along with a red leather waistcoat and top hat) and I would leave home in the Kathleen-approved outfit, then switch gear *à la* Jekyll & Hyde before having to face my peers. Outlandish maybe, but the only way to retain any teenage dignity. Of course, getting out of my clobber under the trees and under cover of darkness at midnight, and dressing again in my ma's attire could be tricky, especially when under the influence of drink and/or other substances. This kind of deceit became much easier when I eventually got my hands around the steering wheel of my father's company car. It was then just a question of sneaking my gear into the boot well in advance of my departure. Inconvenience was the price of appearing trendy. The Kinks' Ray Davies had it sussed in 'Dedicated Follower of Fashion'.

As for promiscuity, there was not much evidence of it in the life of a trained athlete like myself – not for the want of trying, mind you. Football took up most of my time, so partying and pursuing sexual quarry were not that high on the priority list, although I did have my moments. I lost my virginity in the bike shed at school one cold Saturday night after we had been to the pictures. It was all over in a flash with little romance; I am certain I was a great disappointment, although the relationship lasted for a couple of years afterwards.

In the meantime, unknown to me throughout these years of playing with the school team on Saturday mornings and then with grown men in the semi-professional world on Saturday afternoons, Frank Matthews was never far away. Apparently he was keeping himself well informed of my progress, and in the later months of 1966 he approached me with the offer of a trial with English Second Division side, Barnsley. Our school-team skipper, Graham Smith, was also to make the Friday morning journey to Yorkshire by train for two trial games before our return on Sunday night or Monday morning. This trip had my parents' approval but unfortunately we received a call on the Thursday night to tell us the trip was off. Storms had flooded parts of England and the Barnsley trial games had been postponed. I replaced the telephone receiver at the bottom of the stairs and smiled as best I could at my parents to hide my deep disappointment. I knew that the moment was gone, my opportunity drowned in the Yorkshire floods.

What I did not bargain for was Frank's persistence, and his switch of allegiance to First Division Aston Villa, the very club Uncle Bobby Brolly had had a chance to join all those years before me. What was not initially clear to me was the reason Bobby had spurned that opportunity to join Villa. Hindsight reveals it to have been a crucial factor in my parents' decision-making process. Frank Matthews's last stand in our living room and his failure to dissuade my parents from putting my education first came as a devastating blow.

As Frank left for home I quickly disappeared to my bedroom, my insides in turmoil, my mind conjuring with the alternatives that lay before me. What I did not realise at the time, and what only became clear to me a few weeks ago, is that Uncle Bobby had been free to make his own choice when it came to deciding if he fancied a future as a professional footballer with Aston Villa. He had been older than me and his choice was to view football as a wonderful pastime, putting education and a career in the 'real' world before sport.

I now realise that his reasoning heavily influenced my parents, who saw education as the key to a stable future whereas football was a short career, even for those few who survived the apprenticeship and made it into the first team. I can understand that attitude, but I believe that at sixteen years of age I should have been given the opportunity to discover for myself if I had the makings of a professional player. Failure might have hurt but would have come early enough for me to resume my education.

At the time I regarded it as a disappointment. But although I made my own protest, it really did not occur to me that this was my last chance. It is only now when I look back that I feel deep regret, that I realise I should have fought harder for what I wanted. By the time I did come to terms with the reality of my parents' decision, it was too late.

Frank Matthews managed to persuade Jake Findlay's parents to allow him to take his chances at Villa. He signed for them and not only made the first team but almost made it as a Scottish international. I envied Jake Findlay. I might not have made it to the first team, but how I wish I had had the chance to try. As soon as Frank Matthews's car disappeared from our street I made my own rash decisions. My thinking was far from clear but I was determined to exact revenge and careless about the target of my resentment.

Education! I would give them education. I had made my decision privately and it would remain private. So private, in fact, that my mother knew nothing of it for twenty-eight years, until I revealed my protest action to her in the year before her death. Nor did my father know anything. In the run-up to the examinations – I was taking eight O-Levels – I concentrated little on my work and played more football than I ought to have done, and when cornered about studies I simply went to my room and did nothing at all. I would read copies of Charlie Buchan's famous *Football Monthly*, keeping my schoolbooks handy in case of sudden intrusions. When the examinations came I walked in and wrote my name at the top then put a line through each page in a very deliberate act of sabotage, a perfect example of shooting myself in the foot; because when the examination results arrived by mail I felt ashamed of what I had done. But there was no going back – except to repeat my O-Level year – and this time to leave school with six passes.

It was also time to move on. My parents decided to return to live in Northern Ireland in October 1968, five months after Manchester United had won the European Cup at Wembley. It was an opportunity to go back home and I relished the thought, but it also meant we were moving further away from my spiritual home at Old Trafford.

Part II

The Sorrowful Seventies

4

From Civil Rights to Civil Wrongs

It was difficult to tell which of us felt the more uncomfortable. I could rationalise the cause of my own discomfort in the presence of someone at the peak of his fame. George Best was sitting a few feet away, and it was as if he were as embarrassed by my presence as I felt myself. He was shy, down-to-earth, normal, and his folks made me and stills cameraman John Bell very welcome at their home in Burren Way on the Cregagh estate in East Belfast. Here was a man with the world at his feet, playing 'keepie-up' with the globe, an incredibly skilled performer on the pitch, the 1968 European Footballer of the Year, El Beatle, the Prince of Players, the sex symbol whose propulsion into stardom had permanently changed the face of professional football – and here he was chatting quietly to the small-time editor of a low-circulation Belfast weekly paper, *CityWeek*.

It was the summer of 1970, two years after Best had scored the all-important second goal for United when we beat Benfica 4–1 in the European Cup final at Wembley in May 1968. He was willing to talk about anything. There were no conditions laid down when we arranged to have this chat. We talked about winning the European Cup, and I was honest with him when I said I thought John Aston was the star of the show that night for the manner in which he constantly outpaced their defence, making them look lethargic. He agreed it had been an outstanding performance. Then I spoke of the semi-final victory that year over our old enemies Real Madrid. Just as in the 5–1 thrashing of Benfica at the Stadium of Light in 1966, we travelled to Madrid for a second-leg game with a one-goal lead. This was another night of glory for us in Europe. The Spanish champions were 3–1 up at half-time.

'What did Matt Busby say to you at half-time?' I asked. Bestie was at his best in football conversation and his responses were given enthusiastically and with great candour. He told me the 'boss' did not use the interval to slag his team off for conceding three goals and allowing Real Madrid to outplay them in the first half. No matter what pressure Sir Matt was under to bring us European glory as he moved rapidly towards retirement, George said he had simply told his team to 'go back out there and enjoy yourselves.' His attitude was that the team had done well to get this far. Throw caution to the wind and attack. What happened next is forever written into United folklore, and many, myself included, regard this game in Madrid on 15 May 1968 as the 'real' European Cup final.

The power of the United attack tore the Real Madrid defence to shreds in the second half, and with just fifteen minutes to go David Sadler sneaked in to level the scores 3–3 on aggregate, although we were still 3–2 down on the night. Then, inevitably, George Best took control. Receiving the ball from a Pat Crerand throw-in he set off on a glorious run, leaving defenders in his wake, pulling the ball back to the edge of the penalty area at perfect pace for the oncoming Bill Foulkes to side-foot the ball into the net. We had won, and were finally on our way to the elusive European Cup glory that had been Sir Matt Busby's goal in 1956. But for the Munich disaster, victory in Europe would have come long before. George Best had played a major part in righting that wrong.

As I listened to his description of life as an icon I felt that the pressure of such fame was having remarkably little effect on Best. The longer we chatted, the more comfortable I became – and just a little bolder. Would he agree to help me to boost sales of the paper by signing fifty portraits of himself if we got them printed and delivered to the house first thing next morning before he left for Manchester, and would he have time to fill in a questionnaire? We would give the portraits away free to the first fifty names drawn out of a hat.

'No problem,' he said, in a matter-of-fact way. 'You don't have to rush them up tomorrow, I don't go back until the day after.'

I floated out of the Best family home that day. Naturally, I awarded myself one of the portraits, and along with George's handwritten responses to the questionnaire it is carefully stored away among my most prized possessions. They are so well stashed I cannot find them, but I know they are there somewhere. It is a shortcoming of mine to put things away for safety, but then to forget where exactly. One day, when least expected, the George Best memorabilia will turn up to brighten the day.

The trouble with attempting to interview the rich and famous is their unpredictability. It comes of being wealthy, talented and beholden to no one. As a result their tolerance level is greatly diminished. Wealth and fame achieved, they no longer need to court the media. A good many personalities view reporters and photographers with suspicion and disdain in equal amounts. But then, why should we expect to be permitted to force ourselves on an individual just because he or she might make good copy? Even when I get close I feel uncomfortable – as if I am intruding on this individual's space when they could be doing something they really want to do, like sitting in a darkened room writing songs, relaxing before a big game or just spending time with the people they love. George Best, however, displayed neither resentment nor egotism. When I interviewed him he seemed as embarrassed by his success as I was by my hero-worship.

After returning to Northern Ireland with my family in 1968, I flirted briefly with the idea of getting some A-Levels. My intention was to take my examinations as a pupil at Wallace High School in Lisburn as a prelude to attending an agricultural college. It was clear from day one at the school that this plan was unlikely to see fruition. Having come from a comprehensive system at Blairgowrie High School where teachers were prepared to meet you at your own level to discuss sex and drugs, and even to attempt to educate you in the ways of the public house, I found Wallace a culture shock. The authoritarian regime was not to my liking. I endured it for about eight weeks, the end hastened by a run-in with a teacher who objected to my posting our Drinking League Table on one of the school noticeboards.

Without informing my parents, I made moves to find an alternative to school. The answer came from a customer at the filling station near our home where I spent

Sundays pumping petrol. He knew of my disillusionment at school and of my interest in farming, so he pointed out an advertisement in the local paper for a trainee reporter at *FarmWeek*, a Morton Newspapers publication. My parents learned of this dramatic change in direction not from me, unfortunately, but from Hal Crowe, editor of *FarmWeek*, who telephoned the house one day when I was at school to ask if I could start a week earlier than we had agreed. A heated debate followed school that day, but eventually Billy and Kathleen accepted my reasoning. So by December 1968 I was covering local livestock markets to make my living. Me, a vegetarian since I had witnessed the slaughter of pigs from my Uncle Sammy's farm, earning a crust from the sale of animals for slaughter! All for £7 a week.

Ten months later I was on the move to a newspaper in Norwich, with the intention of being closer to Vicki. Our romance had blossomed in my final weeks in Scotland, but Vicki and her family had since moved back to their native England. We got married in 1970 and moved to Belfast, where I had secured a post with Morton Newspapers as editor of *CityWeek*, the opportunity to double my wages to £30 a week being a compelling reason to make the move. Securing the George Best interview and offering his personally signed portraits was a massive success. Circulation almost doubled for the two weeks in which he featured prominently. Without George Best, though, circulation returned to what had become the 'norm', and that – as the company directors were quick to point out – was inadequate if we were to attract more advertising revenue, the life-blood of any paper.

The staff decided to revamp the image of the paper, targeting the teenage market and rechristening it *Thursday*, the day of publication. Once or twice management carpeted me over articles we published, but by and large we were given freedom to try to make this new venture a success. At first we watched joyfully as the circulation climbed slowly but we were devastated to witness a major problem over a centre spread on birth control which included full details on every type of precaution available, including how and where to acquire them. There was less than universal approval among our Catholic newsagents and the consequent refusal of a number of outlets to stock the paper thereafter hurt our chances of making *Thursday* a success. The paper peaked during the early part of the 1970–71 season but died before the season ended, when I left to join the *News Letter* as a reporter. Manchester United's season was even less distinguished; at least *Thursday* did peak.

Without Sir Matt Busby at the helm – he retired on 14 January 1969, six months after the European Cup final victory – United was a rudderless ship. Wilf McGuinness, former player and reserve team coach under Busby, was appointed manager – the kind of 'keeping-it-in-the-family' appointment which has long has been Liverpool's method of maintaining consistency of performance on and off the pitch. In United's case it just did not work. Wilf McGuinness got off to a bad start. Right from the outset the warning signs were there for all to see, that our European champions team was cracking up, with the old and infirm not being adequately replaced by players of quality.

We lost the first three games under McGuinness in the

1969–70 season, and his response for the fourth game was to drop Billy Foulkes, Bobby Charlton, Shay Brennan and Denis Law. Foulkes never played for us again, instead becoming the youth team coach. McGuinness complained that the United board would not fund his attempts to sign the likes of Malcolm McDonald and Mick Mills, although for some reason he did manage to persuade them to buy Arsenal centre-half Ian Ure. Then he had a falling out with George Best, with the result that the Belfast man was suspended for the whole of January, returning in style, mind you, to score six of our eight goals in a fifth-round FA Cup game against Northampton. We finished eighth in the league and lost out in the semi-finals of the FA Cup and the League Cup, to Leeds in the former and to our deadly rivals Manchester City in the latter.

McGuinness's reign as manager ended within a few months of the kick-off of the 1970–71 season and Sir Matt Busby came out of retirement to resume control of his beloved United, with the challenge of finding a suitable manager to restore the glory days. Not even Sir Matt could rediscover the magic touch that had given us so much pleasure in the previous decade, although he did have a stabilising influence and there were some notable games. We drew 4–4 away to Derby, beat Crystal Palace away 5–3 and won the final game of the season away to Manchester City by four goals to three. Once again we finished eighth in the league.

The last edition of *Thursday* was published on 4 March 1971. My weekend was spent playing football for Woodburn Young Men, a Churches League side from Carrickfergus. After the game we rushed to the pub for the football scores. United had lost 4–3 away to West Bromwich Albion, a team supported by the BBC's Ireland Correspondent Denis Murray – someone unknown to me at the time, but who was to become a colleague later, at both the *Belfast Telegraph* and the BBC. Such was the rarity of a West Brom victory over Manchester United, that as recently as 1996 Denis was still recalling the hat-trick by Tony Brown and the single goal by John Wile which led to our defeat.

By the morning of Monday 8 March I had reason to push aside all thoughts of the disappointing result. It was my first day on duty in the *News Letter* newsroom, on a four to midnight shift, and I soon realised that a job in news journalism would require a radical change in life-style. Up until now the civil and political unrest had been going on all around me, yet because I had no direct involvement in covering the distressing events I was somehow able to divorce myself from the reality of what was happening.

My arrival at the *News Letter* coincided with the murders of three young Scottish soldiers on 9 March. They had been shot dead while enjoying an off-duty drink in a pub in the Ligoneil area of North Belfast. As the newcomer I was not given the job of covering the story, but the callous nature of the killings became abundantly clear as the facts began to emerge. The incident marked one of the many 'watersheds' in the campaign of violence which had been gathering momentum since voices were first raised in protest by those for and against the civil rights movement. In the space of a couple of years we had gone from arguing with one another, to shouting and yelling across phalanxes of police officers and British soldiers, to barbaric acts of murder in the cause of Irish republicanism or loyalism. It was a relatively short step from civil rights to civil wrongs. My entry into the world of news journalism coincided with the sound of squabbling being replaced by the deafening noise of explosions and gunfire as Northern Ireland was plunged into the depths of the bloody conflict which has dominated our lives for nearly thirty years now.

In those days Belfast city centre came to a standstill at six o'clock every evening. Buses stopped running at around that time to avoid hijackings later in the evening. Bars, restaurants and cinemas also closed. People rushed home and stayed there, fearful of making any journey which might invite the wrath of the 'other side', frightened of being beaten up or losing vehicles to hijackers. It was eerie walking through the city centre after seven o'clock, occasionally getting an unpleasant whiff of CS gas carried in the night air from the latest hot spot, visible somewhere on the horizon as a pall of black smoke rising from burning vehicles. Often I wouldn't see a soul as I made my way towards the Great Victoria Street railway station. The only noises were those made by my footsteps, the starlings' constant cacophony, and the distant howl of hatred as somewhere on the periphery of downtown Belfast angry mobs vented their anger. Tumbleweed would not have looked out of place.

Of course, with the *News Letter* it was part of my job to cover the civil disturbances on both sides of the religious divide. On these occasions hatred became tangible. 1972 and 1973 were two of the most horrific years of the conflict. 1972 had barely got under way when the Parachute Regiment shot dead thirteen unarmed men in Derry, wounding seventeen others. Bloody Sunday prompted an Official IRA bomb at Aldershot military barracks, home of the 16th Parachute Brigade, killing five women workers, a gardener and a Catholic priest. By March the government had suspended the Stormont Parliament and replaced it with direct rule from Westminster. For a time during the summer the Provisional IRA operated a ceasefire, suspending for two weeks its indiscriminate campaign of car bombings. Meanwhile, the new Secretary of State for Northern Ireland, William Whitelaw, met IRA leaders. The hundredth soldier was killed by a sniper after the talks broke down.

Loyalists began setting up no-go areas, and when a fifteen-year-old boy died after being knocked down by an army vehicle, the UDA opened fire on British soldiers. 21 July witnessed Bloody Friday when the IRA set off twenty-six bombs in Belfast, killing eleven people and injuring 130. On the same day a loyalist gang kidnapped a Catholic and took him to a club in the Shankill Road area where he was beaten, tortured and stabbed repeatedly before being shot and his body dumped. This was the first killing by members of the gang which became known as the Shankill Butchers. In Operation Motorman the Army moved into Catholic areas to remove barricades and loyalists responded by dismantling theirs. By the end of the year 467 people had died in the bloodiest year of the conflict, a year which also witnessed 10,628 shootings and 1,853 bomb attacks.

One of those bombs exploded outside the *News Letter* building in Donegall Street, killing six people, including two police officers who believed they were leading shoppers to safety but who, because of a hoax call from the Provisionals, were actually leading them towards the source of the hundred-pound explosion. Pieces of one of the police officers were found on the roof of the *News Letter* building, immediately outside the attic office I shared. The bomb went off on 20 March, a day I will never forget. There was no warning. A filing cabinet sheltered me from the shards of glass which were blasted into the room. We were completely disoriented by the noise and the flying debris. There were screams and shouts as we tried to establish if everyone was all right. The late Peter Rea was thrown to the floor, and when the dust settled he looked for all the world like a dead man. I pushed him but got no response. Then, taking his head in my lap, I slapped his face, shouting, 'Pete, Pete, speak to me,' and his eyes flickered. He was grey with dust but he was alive, so I went to check the others. Eventually, we helped Pete to his feet (he walked with the aid of a stick following a stroke) and we all set off towards the front door of the building. It was dark in the dust-filled corridors as the features department made its way out of the debris which moments before had been our office. We were met by a hideous sight.

I felt nauseous as I surveyed the scene. There was a large crater in the road directly in front of our office and at the entrance to the shopping arcade opposite. A refuse lorry was parked nearby. People were lying on the ground crying out for help. Police reinforcements were just beginning to arrive along with other rescue services. I saw an elderly man receiving first aid, one of his legs almost completely severed from his body. There was blood all over the pavements, and pieces of flesh. There was a dreadful smell.

My colleagues set off for the local watering hole, the Duke of York. It was a struggle not to add to the pandemonium by bending over to vomit, so I went back inside the building and returned to the top floor. For the next couple of hours I busied myself clearing up the glass, carefully piling it up in the corridor outside, and brushing up the dust. I had almost finished this task when a police officer on the roof of the building looked through our glassless window frame. He was surprised to see me, a little shocked and maybe even angry. He ordered me to leave the building at once as the area had not yet been given the all-clear from army bomb officers. In one hand he held a police officer's cap – clearly not his own – and in the other he had a plastic bag containing a piece of a police officer's tunic. On closer examination I saw the fingers of a severed hand. It took me a matter of seconds to transfer my shocked and shattered body to the pub.

This was not the only explosion I witnessed. A bomb went off one day at the offices of the British Caledonian airline at the corner of Lower Ann Street and Bridge Street as I walked towards it on my way to work. There was no warning. I first saw the flash, then heard the explosion and felt the ground shake. An elderly woman in front of me fell to the pavement, the contents of her shopping bag spilling out as pieces of glass showered down upon us. Her knees were cut, but apart from her tears she seemed to be all right, so once I had helped her to her feet and repacked her shopping bag I resumed my walk to work,

5

THOSE SECOND DIVISION BLUES

Bone crashed on bone and blood spurted from the guy's face as he fell to the ground. Then a sharp pain in the back as a boot made contact. I buckled and turned in time to see a body flash across my range of vision, a fist making contact with a face, presumably the face responsible for the boot in my back. This was the first time I'd become involved in a ruck. Not by choice, you understand; it just happened. It was over quickly, but while it was going on it felt as if everything was happening in slow motion. As we manoeuvred ourselves away from the human debris, blood dripped from my right hand and my scarf was stained with it. Moments before we'd been walking away from the Stretford End towards the city centre, cheering, happy with the fantastic match we had just witnessed – a crucial 3–2 win over Sunderland. The official crowd figure for the game on 30 November 1974 was given as 60,585, but on the Stretford End terracing it was a very tight squeeze that day – so tight that we estimated the crowd was actually closer to 63,000. You could tell the size of the crowd by the tightness of the squeeze.

Manchester United had played the game the way we expected them to play it – dazzlingly brilliant on the attack, and yes, therefore, occasionally vulnerable in defence. Sunderland came to Old Trafford as our closest rivals in the league and with a reputation for attacking past the gaping hole which had once been the British Caledonian office. That is how it was in those days. You just got on with life in the face of extreme violence. Before the day ended, no doubt, the shops next door would have reorganised their stock and posted 'Bomb Damage Sale' notices on the newly fitted glass windows. Once during a particularly heavy series of IRA bombings in the city centre, a shopkeeper near Castle Junction demonstrated the black sense of humour and the spirit of the people when he put up a notice saying: 'Buy now while shops last.'

As 1974 approached, United were heading for Division Two and the Ulster Workers' Council strike was about to drive me away from Belfast.

play. They served up a treat, a game to remember for all time. Never mind which division it was in. Stuart Pearson gave us the lead and then we paid the price for our adventurous play. Sunderland had an outstanding left-winger called Billy Hughes, a George Best lookalike who had the same long black hair and the same free spirit as the Belfast boy. When he had the ball, we worried. He was definitely a United type of player; he should have been signed by the Doc. Hughes scored twice to give Sunderland the lead. In any other circumstances his goals would have been worthy of applause, but they were against us. Even though we were one goal behind at half-time, we still felt confident about the outcome. In the second half the game went from end to end but our defence held, our forwards (Morgan and McIlroy) scored twice and we won 3–2.

Throughout our season in the Second Division when I was a regular on the Stretford End I got to see the same faces every week – and that included the uniformed guards who seemed to think their job was to cause trouble. Many of us became friends but remained nameless throughout our association. Others were known only by their first names – Martin and Big Dave stick out in the memory, and with good reason. Without their help the ruck near Manchester's Piccadilly station would almost certainly have amounted to a mugging, and I would have ended up in hospital or worse. Our journey into town had been interrupted by a small group of Sunderland supporters. It was always difficult to determine who supported whom when our two clubs met, because Sunderland's colours also featured red, white and black. Often it was down to recognising the Geordie accents. On this occasion they should have been kept in the stadium until we had cleared away, except for those who in their desperation to see the game found themselves with tickets into our sections of the ground. The Sunderland fans made it quite clear that they knew we were a group of five, isolated from the main body of United supporters. There was no way out but to confront them and deal with the situation. Having to fight with the Geordies concluded what had been a dreadful week for me in Sheffield – and preceded what was to become an even worse fortnight.

It was during the dark days of the Ulster Workers' Council strike that I made the decision to move the family to Sheffield. As loyalist protest actions against the Sunning-dale agreement and the power-sharing executive began to strengthen, it seemed to me that it was time for a change. So one week in May I bought a copy of the *UK Press Gazette* with its extensive section of jobs for journalists, and set off to scour England, Scotland and even, if necessary, Wales. I travelled by train from Stranraer to Rugby in the Midlands, then to Hereford near the Welsh border, then to Sheffield and finally to Greenock outside Glasgow. I made appointments for interviews from public telephone boxes in the railway stations. I was offered jobs with the *Greenock Telegraph* as sports editor, with the *Rugby Advertiser* also as sports editor, and with *The Star* in Sheffield as a sub-editor in the features department.

We sold our house and moved to Sheffield at the beginning of June 1974. The political climate was such that it seemed the loyalists who established the UWC had a grip on Northern Ireland. The country was facing widescale disruption, with power cuts increasing in frequency, petrol rationed by the Government and threats to the water and sewerage systems. In this volatile atmosphere terrorists filled the political vacuum with acts of barbarity. In February eleven people died when a bomb exploded on a coach carrying servicemen and their families along the M62 near Bradford. The worst of the bombings came on 17 May when twenty-two people died in three car bomb explosions in rush-hour Dublin. More than a hundred others were injured. This was the political background to our move to Yorkshire. To make matters worse, Manchester United had just completed the most humiliating season in their history and were relegated to Division Two for the first time since 1938.

Like Wilf McGuinness, Frank O'Farrell's hold on the management reins at Old Trafford was brief and entirely unsuccessful. He lasted just eighteen months before being replaced by Tommy Docherty in December 1972. With O'Farrell went our wayward genius George Best. By the end of the 1973–74 season all that Docherty's brash, confrontational style of management had achieved was a massive clear-out of the remnants of the 1960s side that had won the European Cup. He gave Denis Law a free transfer to Manchester City in July 1973; Bobby Charlton had disappeared in similar fashion two months earlier to take up the manager's job at Preston North End; Tony Dunne was transferred to Bolton Wanderers in August 1973. Docherty was active on the transfer market, buying in mostly Scottish players, with a sprinkling of Irish. The Scots were George Graham for £120,000 from Arsenal; Alex Forsythe, £100,000 from Partick Thistle;

Lou Macari, £200,000 from Celtic; Jim Holton, £80,000 from Shrewsbury; Stewart Houston, £55,000 from Brentford; Jim McCalliog, £60,000 from Wolves. During the same period Docherty bought Gerry Daly (£22,000) and Mick Martin (£25,000) from Bohemians in Dublin as well as Ray O'Brien (£20,000) and goalkeeper Paddy Roche (£15,000) from Shelbourne. One of the most significant purchases at this time was Stuart Pearson from Hull for £200,000.

The real irony of all this wheeling and dealing was the role of another Scotsman in sending us on our way to Division Two on that dreadful day at Old Trafford, 27 April 1974, when Denis Law came back to haunt us. Law had already announced his retirement and here he was back at Old Trafford in a City shirt for what turned out to be the final game of his career. United had two games left and even victory in both would not necessarily be enough to ensure survival in Division One. The outcome would depend on the results of other sides in the relegation zone. This home game against City was the first of those two remaining fixtures. No scriptwriter could have dreamed up such a dramatic conclusion.

In front of 57,000 spectators, and with eight minutes remaining, the score was 0-0. Then the death blow. The ball bobbled about among a ruck of players in the United goalmouth. Stepney grasped but missed. The ball bounced behind a City player facing away from the United goal. He was just a few yards out from the goal line when he instinctively back-heeled the ball, knocking it agonisingly slowly into the empty net. The scorer did not celebrate. His team-mates did. The City supporters did. He just walked away. Denis Law was deeply distressed by this, his last act as a professional player. Moments later he was substituted by City, an act of kindness for a man who had given his best years in football to Manchester United, a man who really wished he had not scored. The Stretford End invaded the pitch but the result stood and Tommy Docherty wept in the United dressing room as the City scum celebrated our demise.

In the end, Law's goal did not in itself relegate United. Birmingham won at home to Norwich and that ended our hopes of survival. Tears were not far away for me either as I watched the result and the pictures of the invading fans that Saturday afternoon at Bob Stewart's pub near Lambeg – the 'local' for Glebe Swifts players after a game. My team-mate Paul Jones was also a United fan and we drowned our sorrows in our beers, enduring the jeers and taunts of the other Swifts players whose hearts lay at that time with well established First Division sides.

While Docherty went off to prepare for life in the Second Division the UWC strike spurred on my move to Sheffield. Living there took me away from the day-to-day political events unfolding back home but there were times when the Irish problem was brought murderously into focus in England by the IRA. On 5 October 1974, five people died and fifty-four were injured in the Guildford pub bombings and then on 21 November – nine days prior to the Sunderland game – twenty-one people were killed and 182 injured when the IRA set off bombs at two Birmingham pubs. After such atrocities you became very conscious of your Irishness. While the 'war' was being conducted at a safe distance in Ireland there was nothing but sympathy from English people who noticed the accent; but when bombs went off in England warm feelings were quickly replaced by suspicion, and some people developed a simple loathing of all things Irish. I sympathised deeply with those who suffered bereavement or injury.

Just once was I challenged because of my accent, a few days after the Birmingham bombs. It was around seven in the evening as I left a public telephone box near my home in Sheffield. There was a queue outside. As I held the door open for the next man in line, he gave me a look to kill and remarked that perhaps he should search inside the phone box before entering. As I stepped away I told him he had no need to search, he had a full ten minutes to get out! Soon this guy was following me, his call completed in record time, but I lost him eventually by passing my home and travelling a few streets further on. On reflection I regretted what I had said, but I resented being lumped in with terrorists.

Nine days later I found myself part of a small group of United fans followed by Sunderland supporters determined to have a fight. Within a week there would be more trouble involving United fans – and this time it was much closer to home.

Saturday 7 December 1974, when United came to Sheffield Wednesday, is a day I will never forget. That year football in England was beset by crowd disorder, or hooliganism as it was labelled. United did not enjoy a good reputation for away games, although I often felt there was a media bias towards reporting any trouble caused by United fans while ignoring the destructive behaviour of the supporters of other teams, such as Liverpool. My own newspaper, *The Star*, covered the destruction of a train by Liverpool supporters in two paragraphs. Had this been done by United fans it would have made front page headlines. Indeed, I felt so strongly about it I wrote to the editor as a United fan. As you might expect, the letter was not published.

Getting from one side of Sheffield to the other on two bus routes that day was a covert operation. My United colours had to be hidden as I travelled through the city among groups of Sheffield Wednesday supporters in blue and white. It was uncomfortable to say the least, sitting with the enemy. The biggest fear was discovery, attracting attention by not joining the singing or if one sharp-eyed Wednesday fan caught a glimpse of my colours under my jacket. It was imperative to meet up with United fans at some point along the route and slip in among them in the least conspicuous manner possible. I still had to live here after all the United boys had gone home.

United fans were being herded through the city by lines of police officers, many of them on horseback. Some United fans had no police escort and even as we made our way to the game, news of damage to shops was being reported. My colours hidden about my person, I continued on my journey towards Hillsborough, right in among the Wednesday supporters who were by now singing and taunting the United fans being escorted to the ground by the police. It was not until we were within sight of the ground that I made my move, pausing as if looking for someone while the biggest group of Wednesday fans moved on. Then I stepped smartly on to the roadway and came face to face with police officers who initially saw me as one of the Wednesday fans trying to get in to the United party they were escorting. A few United fans were watching me closely, waiting, but when I produced my colours there was a large cheer and I was welcomed into the fold.

We were shepherded by the police towards the Leppings Lane end of the ground – a small terraced area opposite the home supporters' Spion Kop terracing. It was here on 15 April 1989 that ninety-six Liverpool fans died horrifically as they were herded into the ground like cattle, while the police made a complete mess of interpreting the signs of crowd distress. On this day in 1974 they messed up the segregation policy applied by necessity at football grounds the length and breadth of the country. A small number of Wednesday fans had somehow been permitted to enter the area reserved for the visiting support.

The predictable outcome was chaos as the two sets of supporters set about segregating the area themselves. The trouble spilled out on to an area of terracing in the adjoining stand kept free of spectators as a buffer between the United supporters and the Wednesday fans. Fortunately, the trouble on the terraces ended very swiftly and without serious injury, and I managed to avoid becoming involved. More than a hundred were arrested and the Football Association announced it would consider action against both clubs. The net result of their deliberations was to declare that in future United fans must purchase tickets in advance of all away games. Had the authorities taken greater care to ensure total segregation of fans, the Football Association would not have had to sit in judgement on the two clubs.

As for the game itself, it was noteworthy for the 4–4 scoreline, but also for the fact that it was the last game ever played in our first team by one of the United faithful's most idolised players, Jim Holton. Big Jim broke his leg in a tackle with Wednesday's Eric McMordie, who also suffered a broken leg. But what a feast the players served up! United were walloped in the first half, 3–1 down at the interval. But despite losing a fourth goal in the second half we came back to draw the game, giving us a vital point at a crucial stage of the season to ensure our position at the top of League Division Two, a position we occupied from day one of the season right through to the end.

Our first game in Division Two was away to Orient (formerly Leyton Orient, and since restored to their full title), a match watched by 17,772. We won 2–0. Our second game in the campaign was our first at home in the lower division, against Millwall. Their fans had a reputation for troublemaking but on a sunny afternoon in Manchester we took the wind from their sails by beating their side 4–0, three goals coming from Gerry Daly. We had nearly 45,000 supporters inside Old Trafford for that match, an early indication that even though United had been in steady decline since the halcyon days of European glory in 1968, the fans would remain loyal no matter what.

The programme for that first home game against Millwall contained a message from our club chairman, Louis Edwards, acknowledging the 'tremendous support' given during the recent lean years, then almost apologising for the fact that because of the pitch invasion during the match against City the previous April, the club had been compelled to erect fences behind each goal. He warned that fencing would go up all around the ground if there was any attempt to use the unfenced touchline areas to get on to the pitch.

Edwards then turned his attention to the travelling fans at away games:

> It seems to me that many of them think they are defending the honour of the club when they cause trouble but all I can say is there is no credit in being known as the worst behaved football followers in the country. At one time Manchester United supporters had the reputation of understanding and appreciating good football and were always ready to applaud it whether it was from their own team or our opponents. I am very sad when I admit that this reputation no longer applies to Old Trafford. We all want to win but when one team wins then there must be a loser. We have had more than our share of success in the past and recently it has been our turn to be at the other end of the scale. I most earnestly appeal to those responsible for the bad behaviour to think again about your actions and decide to help the club to regain its good name. You can start by cutting out the damage to property and vandalism on the train and coaches and in the cities at away games. We want you to be the best in the country with your vocal support without resorting

to foul language and to show the world that you can be sporting in defeat and modest in victory. Forget the 'United aggro' and makes yourselves the best behaved supporters in the land. If you are unwilling to do this then all I can say is that we don't want you and would prefer to get along without you.

They took our money but they did not want us there if we sang loudly and responded to the taunts of opposing fans with four-letter words. I did not cause damage to property but I did sing in tribal fashion with the others on the Stretford End and there is no denying that the atmosphere in football grounds came from these rival chants.

Louis Edwards's attitude was probably shared by all those who did not have to endure the taunts of rivals and who did not understand what defeat meant to ordinary working lads whose lives centred around their team. When United suffered on the pitch, the main knock-on effect was that their fans suffered off it. I am not trying to justify vandalism or damage to property. I am merely trying to point out that club officials did not appreciate the game in the same way as the guys on the terraces. They did not understand the passion of their supporters. What they should have been doing was to try to find ways of capitalising on the tremendous energy of their fans. There was a feeling that the spectators on the terraces were simply the means of making Manchester United very wealthy. It was as if no one at the club could be bothered to look beyond the turnstile takings. Perhaps board members should have travelled with the fans for a few weeks to arrive at an understanding of their state of mind.

In the same Millwall programme, Tommy Docherty acknowledged the value of the supporters, although he too told the vandals and troublemakers to stay away. But the emphasis was on the fans' positive role, indicating that here was at least one club official who had some rapport with the MU masses:

Welcome back to Old Trafford and our new life in the Second Division. You, the fans, gave us tremendous support in our fight against relegation and I am truly sorry that it did not bring a happier ending. But that battle is now history and I just hope that you will stay with us for the big challenge this season to win promotion. I think I can promise you that the staff and players will make every effort to give you more to cheer about this season. Everyone at Old Trafford is deeply conscious of the debt we owe for your loyal support and it will be our inspiration in the months ahead.

A casual glance at our attendance figures during the season in Division Two reveals just how loyal the United faithful were in the face of failure to remain in the top flight. United was the best supported team in English football, better than any of the First Division sides. A total of 1,016,163 paying customers watched United at Old Trafford, an average home gate of 48,388. Liverpool were closest to this achievement with 965,286 spectators for their home games, an average of 45,966. We have always

had better support than any other team in English football. Sadly, all too often it was the only area in which we
were better than the Scousers! In United's Division Two
season I was a regular attender. Attending home games
was an unexpected pleasure during that astonishing
season and it took a little adjustment on my part to
believe that I was finally close enough to the Theatre of
Dreams to become one of its turnstile customers.

The spirit of the fans on the terracing was fantastic.
They did deliberately set out to taunt visiting spectators.
So what, that was part of the joy of being there. It was
an opportunity to let off steam. It was these lads who
made football such an exciting spectacle, who sang their
hearts out week after week, even in the face of adversity.
Yet it was these same lads who were treated like scum
by the football club, the authorities and especially by the
police.

Before I became a regular at Old Trafford my views
would have been quite different. Never would I have
apportioned any blame to the police or to the football
clubs for their contribution to hooliganism. But once I got
inside Old Trafford for the first time I knew exactly where
I wanted to be for future games. My first visit to the
ground had been from Belfast on 22 January 1972 to see
United play Chelsea. I was twenty-one years of age and
married with a child, and yet I approached Old Trafford
with a feeling of anticipation akin to that which children
feel as they go to bed on Christmas Eve. I wolfed down
breakfast in a greasy diner and pressed my friend Trevor
to get a move on, we had to get to the ground. Mind you,
as it was only ten o'clock in the morning, he was less

inclined to hurry. Eventually we walked towards the stadium, down Warwick Road, and then ... and then ... the moment of truth as we reached the front of Old Trafford. Finally I was standing on the forecourt of the greatest club in the world. I felt I knew the place so well, as if I had been here many times before, that I was on first name terms with players. The reality was disappointing. No one knew me. I was just one of thousands milling about outside the stadium at eleven on the morning of a match with a three o'clock kick-off.

There was a long queue outside the souvenir shop where I bought a Manchester United rug and lampshade for Jason's bedroom at home. I stood in awe at some of the merchandise on sale. Even then I had a feeling that there was a big market for this stuff, before the club twigged on. Remember I had written to them in the 1960s looking for a Manchester United shirt. If only I had had the business acumen to arrange the franchise! The quality of stuff on sale nowadays is vastly improved and, of course, so is the profit. The club always claimed this money was to provide the funds for a championship-winning team, but throughout the 1970s and 1980s that plan clearly never reached fruition.

On my first visit to Old Trafford my friend Trevor, a Chelsea fan, was reluctant to go on the terracing, especially at the Stretford End, so I unsuspectingly had a view of things to come. We bought stand tickets, our seats located on the half-way line but high above the pitch and directly above the directors' box. Aside from losing 1-0 to an Osgood goal, for me the enjoyment of the game was spoiled by being in the seated area. There was simply no atmosphere in our sector, no sustained singing, only applause, polite at that, and the occasional cry of 'U-nit-ed . . . U-nit-ed!'

From our lofty peak we could see the activity on the Stretford End. How I longed to be away from the comfort of these seats to where fans were crammed together, where even the crush barriers could become instruments of pain if you were unfortunate enough to be pinned against them during moments of excitement. Goals could send you hurtling forward and sideways in the same motion, making it almost impossible to keep your footing. Hugging your neighbour, whoever he was, was often the only way of staying upright and then when the moment of celebration had passed you would find yourself miles away from your starting point on the terrace. But in spite of the discomfort, the terraces were the only place to be.

Nowadays, in the wake of the Hillsborough disaster report, all-seater stadia mean that the atmosphere at many grounds has been totally destroyed. The Stretford End offered its customers little in the way of comfort. The toilets were inadequate and smelly, the catering poor and the overwhelming impression was that the club wanted your money but was disinclined to provide proper facilities. The terrace fans were expected to behave like animals and were treated as such. No thought was given to the proposition that if you treated these spectators better then you might expect better from them.

To comply with European regulations spectators began to be fenced in, and the unwillingness to open the fencing at the Leppings Lane end of Hillsborough contributed to the deaths of the ninety-six spectators there. That whole complacent system of ground safety died with them, a system created over years of mismanagement and complicity in that mismanagement by all the responsible authorities – the clubs, the police, local authorities, the government – and by the fans themselves. It will be of little comfort to the bereaved families to know that these deaths did finally focus attention on the appalling treatment of football fans, who had become accustomed to forsaking all rights when they donned a football scarf and climbed the terraces. As Lord Justice Taylor's report was to acknowledge, each of the system breakdowns which brought about the Hillsborough disaster had happened before – at other grounds as well as on one previous occasion at Hillsborough. Of course, as United battled honourably for the Second Division championship, sometimes in front of crowds of more than 60,000, the Hillsborough disaster was still fourteen years away.

Once I had seen United safely back into the top division, it was time for another move, this time back to work in Northern Ireland, as news sub-editor on the *Belfast Telegraph*. Even though Sheffield provided a home base close to the Theatre of Dreams, this was of itself insufficient reason to remain. There was too much missing from life there. No soda bread. No potato bread. No crack at work. It was all about keeping up with the Joneses and having a career plan which occupied your whole life to the point where you didn't have time for a chat and a few jokes. Almost everyone took their lives and careers very seriously indeed. Most of the journalists I worked with had an elevated view of their profession. I just saw it as a way of making a living.

Two of my office colleagues and football team-mates asked me to join them one evening for a night on the town. Their wives were holding a meeting in one of their homes and they thought it might be a good opportunity to get out for a beer. They would call for me at 8.30 pm They arrived at 9.30. I was home by 11 pm. We had three pints! Still, they were good guys and whatever it was inside me pulling me back towards my homeland, it was not because anyone was rude, unkind or uncaring. Towards the end of my time in England, such was my desperation to get home that I travelled to Belfast for an interview for a job in public relations. I was offered the job but decided that it was probably the worst career move I could make if I ever wanted to work in newspapers again. Working as a press officer for the British Ministry of Defence in Lisburn might have offered job security and a career structure, but it would have been committing journalistic hari-kari. The offer from the *Telegraph* was timely and provided a welcome solution to my homesickness.

6

'STRIP, SIR, AND BEND OVER'

Sunday 14 August 1977, and surrounded by Suffolk police officers, I was facing humiliation. They wanted me to remove all my clothing so they could search up my arse for a missing wallet! At the time of my arrest and detention, there seemed to be a whiff of prejudice against anyone with an Irish accent.

It all began with a working assignment to cover for the *Sunday News* the traditional curtain-raiser for the new football season, the Charity Shield at Wembley, where the previous season's League Champions play the FA Cup winners. On Saturday 13 August 1977, I travelled to London to report on Manchester United (FA Cup winners) playing Liverpool (League Champions).

It was a repeat of the journey I had made a few months earlier when the *Sunday News* asked me to cover the FA Cup final between the same sides. Although I was a news reporter with the *News Letter*, the Northern Ireland daily, I also covered sport for the company's sister paper, the *Sunday News*. The sports editor, Colin McAlpin, encouraged me to use the system to my advantage when it came to seeing United at Wembley. He suggested that 'we' (i.e. the *Sunday News*) should apply for a press ticket to the 1977 final. 'We' succeeded. 'We' even managed to get another ticket for my brother Geoff who lived in England at the time. Geoff and I met up in London for a few pints before the game – choosing totally at random a small pub in

Notting Hill which appeared to have a mainly Irish clientèle. There were pictures of Manchester United and Celtic in the bar, and it was a pub I would return to on future Wembley sorties with United. Geoff and I mingled with supporters from Manchester, easily falling into conversation about our club and its ups and downs: the disappointment of the previous year's final against Southampton; Tommy Docherty being a Wembley 'scud', a northern term for a bad luck charm. We speculated that he might be destined never to win under the twin towers. Docherty had been to Wembley five times as a player (four times with Scotland and with Preston in the 1954 final) and twice as a manager (of Chelsea in 1967 and United in 1976), and not once did any of his sides emerge victorious.

Our main aim that day, however, was to destroy Liverpool's chances of achieving something unique. A week earlier Liverpool had clinched the league title for the second successive season – the first time any side had achieved that since Wolves in 1959. Now they needed victory against United to clinch the Double of league and cup, and they still had the European Cup final four days ahead in Rome against Borussia Münchengladbach. As Geoff and I sat in Notting Hill having a few pints, we were bracing ourselves for a tough battle against the Scousers, who were on target for a terrific treble of league, FA Cup and European Cup. We saw few Liverpool supporters as we made our way to Wembley on the tube singing loudly about Manchester United being magic.

Walking up towards the most famous soccer stadium in British football (even if not always regarded as the best or most comfortable), we mingled freely with Liverpool supporters – each side singing, cheering and clapping loudly. When we got inside the stadium there was still time for a couple of pints before we parted to make our way to our seats, Geoff in the stand and me in the press box, where I could see the game but could not according to protocol show any colours or demonstrate any favour to one side or the other.

I packed my scarves into a plastic shopping bag and viewed the spectacle in silence, but bursting into song inside and mouthing the words sung by the United faithful outside my glass tower. The experience was akin to seeing a game from inside one of those executive boxes which have become such a feature of football grounds, where the well-heeled watch the game in total silence as they nibble smoked salmon and caviar and drink champagne. It is only post-Taylor Report that we can fully appreciate that without the noisy, boisterous singing of rival fans, football games may be safer but there is absolutely no atmosphere. The affluent who occupy the all-seater stadia these days would regard it as uncouth to sing and cheer and chant support for their team.

Inside the press box, I settled down with pen and notebook – a page set to one side with the teams listed. This is the way they lined up:

Liverpool: Clemence; Neal, Jones, Smith, Kennedy, Hughes, Keegan, Case, Heighway, Johnson (sub. Callaghan), McDermott
Manchester United: Stepney; Nicholl, Albiston, McIlroy, Greenhoff B., Buchan, Coppell, Greenhoff J., Pearson, Macari, Hill (sub. McCreery)

As arranged, we all met up for a beer at half-time, with the match still scoreless. There was plenty to talk about. It had been a good game with both teams committed to attacking play. We were still enjoying our last pint when there was an enormous roar from the crowd. The game had re-started and someone had scored!

We gulped back the dregs and ran for our seats. There I was at Wembley, supposed to be covering the game, and I had missed the first goal. Some of the other reporters briefed me on what had happened: Stuart Pearson had scored with a shot from just inside the Liverpool penalty area. The ball had been passed to him by Jimmy Green-hoff. I was still scribbling furiously when Liverpool equalised. And what a goal! Jimmy Case got the ball just outside the penalty area, tapped it over the head of onrushing United defender Martin Buchan, and swivelled to volley home in spectacular fashion past the startled Alex Stepney, the ball billowing high into the net. United's lead had lasted for just two minutes. It had been an interesting tactical struggle in the first half with neither side lacking in commitment, but now we would have a different kind of battle for the remaining thirty-five minutes.

Five minutes after Liverpool's equaliser came the winner from United. It was assisted by a touch of good fortune. A cross on the right was dropping towards Liverpool's hard man Tommy Smith and he looked as if he had the situation under control but then Jimmy Greenhoff went in to tackle him. As they staggered with the impact of the challenge, the ball broke free to the on-coming Lou Macari who hit it on the move. It was no real threat to the Liverpool keeper Ray Clemence, who was moving comfortably to cover his goal but the ball struck the reeling Greenhoff and was deflected into the net. The remainder of the game was top-class entertainment with scoring chances on both sides. Case in particular had a couple of good chances but United gathered their troops and steadied for the last thirty minutes to keep their goal unbreached. How did I describe the game in the match report? Without bias, of course, as you can see for yourself:

Doc's Red Army Wrecks Liverpool's Treble Hope

Salute tantalising Tommy Docherty's treble-busting Manchester United. For along with the Champions Liverpool yesterday, they 'crowned' this special Silver Jubilee FA Cup Final with a feast of football fit to set before a Queen. The 1977 Cup final was a tale of two cities – and two red armies. But magnificent Manchester majestically toppled Liverpool, giving manager Bob Paisley little time to find a way of motivating his disheartened players to European Cup glory next Wednesday in Rome. And it was a game of seemingly endless moments of excitement which provided the setting for the coronation of a new king with an age-old name, King Arthur. For it was a performance of 19-year-old Scotsman Arthur Albiston which epitomised the spirit of a United team determined to destroy memories of last year's humiliation at the hands of Second Division Southampton. The young Scot played a major part in stifling the threat from Liverpool's Steve Heighway and Jimmy Case, inspiring his fellow defenders and forwards to a 2-1 victory.

That's fair and impartial, is it not? I also praised the spirit of the game, noting that at the end our manager Tommy Docherty came on and shook hands with each of the disappointed Liverpool players sitting on the pitch, heads bowed, bodies drained. The players applauded each other at the end, and the Liverpool players took the trouble to seek out Stewart Houston, our regular left-back who had injured an ankle two weeks before the final, leaving him in plaster and walking on crutches. The United players delayed their lap of honour until Liverpool had received their losers' medals.

My report concluded: 'Liverpool and Manchester can be two proud cities. For they served up a game which has given new hope for the future of English soccer.' Bob Paisley did enough to get his great team in tune four days later in Rome. They beat the German side 3-1 to win the European Cup, becoming the second English side to win it (Manchester United were the first in 1968, the year after Glasgow Celtic had become the first British team to win it).

While Liverpool fans spent the summer basking in the glory of their side's achievement in winning the league title and the European Cup, we United fans were busy doing what had become all too familiar during close-season after close-season – dreaming of the day when we would finally produce a side with sufficient staying power to win the league. Beating Liverpool at Wembley gave us hope that the young side Tommy Docherty had built in Division Two might just be reaching the kind of maturity needed to challenge for the major honours. They certainly played a wonderful brand of attacking, entertaining football when they were 'on song'. Since returning from the Second Division, they had finished third and sixth in Division One. Coincidentally, during this period we had quite a number of Belfast-born players in the first team squad – Jimmy Nicholl, Sammy McIlroy, David McCreery, Tommy Jackson and Chris McGrath. We watched the papers for details of any new signings the Doc might make to strengthen the squad, but instead we got a scandal which once again took Manchester United off the sports pages and on to the front of every English daily . . . The Doc had been playing away!

Almost before the FA Cup had been put in the trophy cabinet at Old Trafford, a gift-wrapped scandal for the tabloid press – Tommy Docherty admitted that he had been having an affair with the wife of the club's physiotherapist, Laurie Brown. The disclosure threw our club into turmoil. Doc's team was popular with the fans, and the view from our position on the Stretford End was that his team played 'the Man United way' – open, attacking, red-devil-may-care football at one hundred miles per hour. It was so hectic on the pitch at times that we reckoned the opposition got tired out just from watching the team as it buzzed all over Old Trafford like angry wasps pursuing an enemy. Sometimes they came unstuck, but even in defeat it was fun to watch eleven men play at so fast and furious a pace.

Now in June 1977 there was concern that Doc's job was at risk because of his indiscretion. The club issued a statement that there was no plan to change the management. The Stretford End sighed with relief. The Doc announced that he would be leaving his wife to set up home with Mary Brown and for a couple of weeks tabloid attention turned elsewhere. The fuss was dying down as the Browns and Dochertys readjusted their lives. Then we were back on the front pages again, this time because of the activities of the Old Trafford board of directors. Following an emergency meeting at the home of Louis Edwards, the directors issued a statement announcing Docherty's dismissal because he had been 'in breach of the terms of his contract.' United had succumbed to pressure. 'I've been punished for falling in love,' said the forty-nine-year-old Glaswegian. Of course, there was the problem of what should happen if Docherty remained in charge. Would Laurie Brown leave or would he face the sack? United felt they could hardly get rid of the man who appeared to be the innocent victim of events.

One story identified the directors' wives as the source of pressure to have Docherty removed. Another said the Church of Rome had intervened to save the moral soul of Manchester United. Whatever the real reason for the about-face by the United board, the dismissal of Docherty put back even further the day when we would have a team to challenge the best in the league. His successor won nothing, perhaps because he was quick to dismantle the Doc's legacy, his flamboyant and entertaining team. Docherty was a shrewd operator on the transfer market and among his first purchases were Lou Macari from Celtic and Jim Holton from Shrewsbury. Holton became one of the Stretford End's greatest ever heroes. His anthem from the faithful was: 'Six foot two, eyes of blue, big Jim Holton's after you.' Docherty also gave us Steve

Coppell and Gordon Hill to stun defenders with pace and dazzling wing play, servicing Stuart Pearson at centre-forward. This was the team to lead us into the 1977–78 season, the team I went to see play Liverpool at Wembley on 13 August 1977. Dave Sexton may have been our new manager, but it was Tommy Docherty's team he led out that day.

This Wembley trip was the start of a family holiday with my first wife's parents at their home in Norwich. We flew to Heathrow and took a train to Euston where we were met by my father-in-law and his son Nicholas, a sixteen-year-old Norwich City supporter who had accepted my invitation to make his first visit to Wembley. We had breakfast before Vicki took our two sons on to Norwich with her father. Nicholas and I set off 'sightseeing' at that wee pub in Notting Hill before kick-off. Like my brother three months earlier, Nick went to his seat while I went to the press box. A dull game finished 0–0. Before I filed my report we went to the press bar for a few drinks with Derek Waugh, a reporter with a Kettering paper. By seven that evening we were ready for the hundred-mile journey to Norwich – hitching. I have no idea why we hitched, and what a disaster it turned out to be.

On the advice of a London bobby we set off by train towards Ilford. There we started hitching on the A-12 Ipswich road. It took us ages to get a lift, and even then it was only as far as Chelmsford. By now it was nearly midnight. We found a public telephone, and while I continued to stick my thumb out, Nick called the family in Norwich to let them know we were safe and well but struggling to get a lift (it never occurred to me that my

Manchester United scarf might be the reason drivers were so reluctant to stop). But we were in good spirits and we shared the same sense of humour, so the jokes and stories kept us occupied as we trudged on.

It took us all night, walking and getting lifts, to reach Norwich. One driver had picked us up at about five in the morning. I turned around at one point and saw a khaki army uniform on the back seat and realised that we had been picked up by a British soldier. He brought us as far as Ipswich with very little conversation, and we got out and began the walk through the centre of town north-wards towards Norwich. A police car pulled up about a hundred yards ahead of us and a cop got out and blocked the pavement, asking us for our names and addresses. I was still wearing Manchester United colours and carrying a plastic bag containing match programmes. Once the policeman had looked inside the bag he told us to go on.

At the end of our final lift we were dropped right at the top of College Road, where Nick lived with my in-laws. The birds were singing loudly as we wandered beneath the leafy trees on the avenue. We joked about our experi-ence and how it would be the source of much fun for many years to come. When we were fifteen yards short of Nick's front door, two guys got out of a car just as we approached. Their body language told me immediately that they had been waiting for our arrival.

'Mr Moore?' says one.

'Aye, that's me,' says I, 'and I wonder who you might be?'

'We would like you to accompany us to Norwich police headquarters for questioning about a stolen wallet,' said one of the cops.

'Not just at the moment,' I said. 'I'm going in there.' I pointed towards the door of Number 89.

He stepped in front of me, gesturing towards the car.

'We've been out all night hitching a lift from London and I intend to see my family before I go to the police station with you. Unless, of course, you are going to arrest me here and now. Are you?'

We went inside, making certain we remained in full sight of the cops at all times. I had already decided I would no longer communicate with Nick so that they would not be able to say we exchanged information. At the cop station we were questioned in separate rooms. As a juvenile, Nick had his father present throughout. I was on my own with a couple of CID men. Their opening question told me why I was there and why they appeared to have a guard posted at the rear entrance to the station as we were driven inside the gates.

'A soldier's wallet and warrant card would be worth quite a bit in Belfast, wouldn't it?'

I told him I had no idea as I had never tried to sell such items. They pursued this line of enquiry for some time and told me finally that the Ipswich police had requested my arrest and detention until they could get a squad car up to collect me and take me back to Ipswich. By now it was 11.30 am on Sunday 14 August.

They took me to a cell. I was allowed to speak to my father-in-law in front of two officers. He said Nick was tired but seemed to be holding up all right. I told Arthur we had nothing to hide and asked him to get in touch with my friend and fellow *News Letter* news editor in Belfast, Jim McDowell, to ask him to get the National Union of

Journalists on the case. The cops took my personal belongings, including my NUJ press card, which is recognised by all police constabularies. When I arrived at my cell, they removed my shoes and belt and even took my cigarettes, which were placed on a chair outside my cell door. If I wanted to smoke I would have to ring the bell. They offered food; I declined. They locked the door and left. Within minutes I was fast asleep on the blanket-covered mattress – the only furniture in the room, apart from the toilet bowl. It was an easy sleep, much needed after forty-eight hours on the move.

At 3.05 in the afternoon I was wakened by the opening of the cell door. A uniformed cop handed over my shoes and belt and told me to put them back on. As I left the cell on the way to the duty sergeant's office, I collected my cigarettes and lighter. I had been in the duty office for just a few minutes when Nick was brought in. As he sat down beside me he began to say something to me. I placed my finger over my lips to indicate that we should remain silent. The Ipswich cops had arrived. They drove us to Ipswich and ordered us to get out and wait while one of them tore the police car apart, pulling the back seat out of the vehicle and searching everywhere – presumably for the allegedly stolen wallet which they suspected me of hiding during the drive south from Norwich.

Inside, my belongings were tipped out by a uniformed officer on to a large table in an interview room. One of the policemen who had brought us from Norwich ordered me to stand up and he searched me – the third time I had been searched since being taken into custody. It was an aggressive search. Finding nothing, he grabbed my shoulders. 'Take all your fucking clothes off,' he shouted.

Jesus, what?

'Get them off,' he ordered.

I stripped. The policeman picked up my jumper, shoes and trousers. He searched them – again! He checked the lining in every item. Jesus, I thought, he is surely mistaking me for Paul Daniels. When he realised there was no wallet in my shoes, or in the lining of my clothing, he turned to face me.

'Turn round,' he said.

I hesitated. He grabbed my left arm and turned me away from him.

'Bend over,' he bellowed.

Fuck, he wanted to look up my arse. I bent over.

After I had got dressed, the policeman took me to a cell and I slept some more. Later, in an interview room, I demanded to hear the soldier's statement. I listened intently and said there were a couple of points I wanted to clarify. Firstly, the soldier did not describe me very accurately, with no mention of the fact that I was bedecked in two Manchester United scarves. He also described me as having a 'soft Southern' accent. What did the policemen think he meant by that?

One of them said: 'He meant southern English.'

'Do you regard my accent as southern English?' I asked. It was like watching a penny drop from a very great height.

Then the soldier said his wallet had been positioned in the compartment on the central console, immediately in front of the gearstick. There was, of course, no wallet there during my time in the car. But he told the police my opportunity to remove the wallet came when I opened a large road map which for a time covered the gearstick and the central console. I asked the policemen if they could show me the map in question. Blank looks all round

'Did you not want it for fingerprinting?' I asked.

Again, blank looks. I told them the soldier was lying. I had not opened a large map but a road atlas measuring about ten inches by twelve that barely covered my lap. I told them to get the soldier to provide the map and check it for my fingerprints. They said he had left for Germany on a sailing out of Felixstowe.

After I wrote out my own statement the cops told me that the station had received calls from my editor and colleagues in Belfast and from a couple of police officers there, including Harry McCormick, who worked at that time in the RUC press office and who vouched for me. (Sadly, Harry died a short time later.)

The Suffolk police dropped the case and a few months later I decided I didn't want the hassle of proceeding with my complaint against them. Liverpool against Manchester United in the 1977 Charity Shield was one of those games which would live forever in the memory, but not for the quality of the football.

There was not much else of note in the Dave Sexton years at Old Trafford. The fact that he had turned the United job down six years earlier in favour of Queen's Park Rangers did not endear him to many on the terraces, and his style of management was in complete contrast to that of the loud and brash Docherty. In his first season we finished a pitiful tenth in the league and suffered humiliation in all cup trophies. Arsenal beat us 3-2 at Highbury in the second round of the League Cup and we lost by the same score in the fourth round of the FA Cup, this time away to West Bromwich Albion in a replay after a 1-1 draw at home. In the European Cup Winners' Cup we were forced to play our first-round home game against St Etienne of France at Plymouth because of crowd hooliganism at the first leg in France. A 1-1 draw in France was followed by a 2-0 win in Plymouth. But in the next round we lost 4-0 away to FC Porto, in a game played on 19 October, a week before my twenty-seventh birthday.

During the same week Liverpool opened their defence of the European Cup with a 5-1 win over Dynamo Dresden at Anfield and I watched Juventus play Glentoran at the Oval in Belfast. Glentoran did Irish football proud. They held the mighty Juventus to just one goal, Causio scoring for the visitors. The East Belfast club's supporters could hold their heads high, which is more than I could manage.

However, in the European return leg at Old Trafford on 2 November, my pride in United was more than restored. They laid seige to the Porto goal and managed to score five times. Unfortunately, our attacking performance left gaps in defence which were twice exploited by the Portuguese so we ended up going out of the tournament with an aggregate score of 6-5.

Liverpool's Euro-campaign progressed towards an appearance in the final at Wembley on 10 May 1978. That was the day a republican prisoner, Brian Maguire, was found hanged in a cell at Castlereagh holding centre. The police said it was suicide but his death led to street disturbances which went on for a couple of nights. Not that I saw any of the rioting. The *News Letter* sent me to London with the Liverpool hordes to provide a colour story about the large number of Northern Irish fans going to the match. They saw their side win the trophy for the second year in succession, beating the Belgian team FC Bruges 1-0. It was the worst assignment of my life, surrounded as I was for over twenty-four hours by screaming Scousers and even worse, standing on the terracing behind the goal where Dalglish scored the winner and being compelled by force of numbers to jump and cheer.

It was galling to see Liverpool continuing to dominate while United struggled. More worrying was the growing evidence that United's attacking style of play was being abandoned in favour of Sexton's more methodical, measured system. Frankly it was dull fare, coming so soon after Docherty's full-blooded approach, and his ability to build an attacking force that entertained, even in defeat. Sexton gave us a team that may have been more efficient but was far too cautious to catch the eye. The players were scared to risk putting individuality above the team effort. Sexton's possession game could best be described as 'sideways football'. Players blessed with attacking skills would elect to pass sideways or backwards rather than risk losing possession. There was no room in Sexton's set-up for players with individual, match-winning flair such as Gordon Hill.

Sexton's first brief flirtation with glory, or should I say almost glory, came with our progress to the 1979 FA Cup final against Arsenal. Sexton had brought in Joe Jordan and Gordon McQueen from Leeds for £350,000 and £500,000 respectively. Mickey Thomas came from Wrexham for £300,000. Many players from the Docherty era remained – Arthur Albiston, Jimmy Nicholl, Jimmy Greenhoff, Sammy McIlroy, Steve Coppell and Lou Macari. This was the nucleus of the side which took us to Wembley with victories over Chelsea, Fulham, Colchester, Tottenham and Liverpool (in a semi-final replay). 12 May 1979 was cup final day and it was the occasion I chose to take my son Jason to his first United game. He was nine years old. On the train to the twin towers, Jason was given permission, for this day only, to join in the singing of United songs which had a few words nine-year-olds would not normally have in their vocabulary – on condition that he would not tell his mother! The sun shone brightly on Wembley that day, but our performance did not match. The team looked decidedly uncomfortable on the ball and unsure of the application of Sexton's tactics. Thank God Jason was with me because at least there was the pleasure of watching his eyes glint with excitement.

It was a poor game, made memorable only because United fought back from being two goals down. With four minutes left we looked a jaded and beaten side, until McQueen stretched out his leg to send the ball wide of Pat Jennings into the Arsenal goal. Sitting in the press box, my friend Peter McCusker and I just managed to avoid jumping for joy at this late strike. Two minutes later Sammy McIlroy wriggled into the penalty box and somehow managed to push the ball past Jennings. Suddenly it was 2–2. Now it was impossible for Peter and me to contain ourselves. We were on our feet, banging the low roof of the press box and sending large pieces of rusty girder flaking down on top of the other hacks. But while we were still celebrating this great recovery and believing for the first time since the kick-off that we could win the cup in extra time, Arsenal's Alan Sunderland got to a Graham Rix cross on our goal line and forced the ball home to give the Gunners a 3–2 victory. We may not have realised it at the time, but it was a sign of things to come during Sexton's years in office – the promising build-up of foreplay but the inability to reach a satisfactory climax.

So much for Sexton's sideways football theory. He lasted only four years, peaking in the 1979–80 season when we finished second in the league, two points adrift of our arch rivals Liverpool. Briefly, the league title looked as though it was within our grasp, especially after we beat Liverpool 2–1 at home in April in front of 57,342 spectators.

At the start of that season, in August 1979, I made a major career move, switching from the print media to broadcasting. My first official day as a BBC employee was destined to become one of the most notorious in the Northern Ireland conflict. It was a bank holiday weekend. On the Saturday United played away to Arsenal, our third game of the new season, drawing 0–0. We were sixth in the league and I was extremely hungover after my *News Letter* farewell party the night before. I woke up in my mother's house in Lisburn, unclear as to why and how I had arrived there.

At least I had an extra day to recover before starting my new job. The BBC told me not to turn up on bank holiday Monday, 27 August, as there would be a very short evening news bulletin.

So that morning Vicki and I packed a picnic and set off for a drive around the Mournes, pausing briefly in Newcastle to visit the amusements and have a bit of a kick-about. At just seven months, my daughter Louise was restricted to viewing the world from her pram. Then it was into the hills on the mountain route out of Newcastle heading towards Kilkeel. We had our picnic on a hillside near the Silent Valley reservoir but the silence was broken by the sound of a loud explosion. As we were speculating that it must have come from a quarry somewhere, there was a second explosion. It was not until we returned home just after nine that evening that we discovered the real source of the explosions.

The news was delivered in such a tactless fashion that I wondered how my new employers could be so insensitive. The first twenty minutes concerned the murder earlier that day of Lord Mountbatten at Mullaghmore in County Sligo. His fourteen-year-old grandson, a seventeen-year-old boatman and the Dowager Lady Brabourne also died in the IRA attack. Then, after twenty minutes and almost, it seemed, as an afterthought, the newsreader got around to telling us that sixteen soldiers (the death toll rose later to eighteen) had been killed in two explosions at Narrow Water near Warrenpoint. A few weeks later one of the BBC's London bosses on a visit to Belfast asked me how I was settling in and I told him I felt ashamed of the BBC for their coverage of the deaths of the eighteen soldiers. He admitted that a mistake had been made and said it would never be repeated. Three soldiers died when I joined the *News Letter* in 1971 and now twenty-two people had died on my first day with the BBC.

PART III

THE EXASPERATING EIGHTIES

7

SHOOTING IN THE CEMETERY

The face was leaner than that seen by millions on television that notorious March afternoon. The hair was long and greying, tied in a ponytail. The face smiled as it leaned towards me across the table and said: 'Tell your cameraman I am sorry I took a pop at him. It's just that I could only see a silhouette against the skyline from where I was and it looked as though some Provo was raising something on to his shoulder to fire at me.' Well there was no doubt our cameraman Peter Cooper was 'shooting' Michael Stone as he fled from the murderous havoc he had created in Milltown Cemetery in west Belfast. Eighteen months later I met Stone during a visit to the Maze Prison sponsored by the Northern Ireland Office and the Prisons Service some time during the summer or early autumn of 1989. It was the first time I had seen him since 16 March 1988 when he had bombed and shot his way out of Milltown during the funerals of the three IRA members shot dead by the SAS in Gibraltar – Sean Savage, Mairéad Farrell and Daniel McCann.

About ten minutes before Stone began tossing grenades at the crowd of mourners, I had spoken to our news desk on the two-way radios we used to maintain contact in the Belfast area. (Mobile phones were not yet in vogue.) My message as we entered the cemetery was that the funerals had passed off without incident up to this point and it looked as though we could expect to fill a smaller portion of the programme than we might have anticipated.

In the year prior to these IRA funerals there had been a series of severe clashes between mourners and the RUC and British soldiers. Perhaps the best example of this problem was the funeral in April 1987 of leading IRA man Lawrence Marley, a key figure in the planning of the 1983 Maze Prison escape, who was shot dead by the UVF. Marley's house in the Ardoyne area of Belfast was surrounded by police and soldiers, the whole area saturated in an attempt to prevent an IRA show of strength. Uniformed RUC officers lined either side of the street from the gateway to the Marley home, creating a kind of corridor for the cortège to pass through. Several times over a period of days the coffin came out of the house, only to be carried back in again.

This RUC tactic was discussed by the British and Irish governments, and following a meeting of the inter-governmental conference at Stormont on 22 April a statement was issued saying there was a need for more sensitive policing by the RUC of paramilitary funerals. However, similar tactics were employed later in the year during the funerals of eight IRA men shot dead by the SAS during a bomb attack on Loughall RUC station in County Armagh. By the time it came to the funerals of the Gibraltar three, it appeared that both sides realised the need to pull back from the constant clashes. Certainly, by the time I was heading towards west Belfast for the funerals of Savage, McCann and Farrell on 16 March 1988 the RUC policy seemed to have been dramatically altered. Gone was the heavy presence of police and soldiers, hence my comment to the BBC newsroom as we entered Milltown Cemetery. Moments before, I had interviewed one of the lawyers walking behind the cortège to observe RUC tactics that day, Pat Finucane, who would be dead before a year had passed, a victim of the UFF. He died on 12 February 1989, about a week before Stone's trial got under way. As we approached the cemetery Finucane was telling me he was delighted that common sense had prevailed on both sides.

The funerals of the Gibraltar active service unit of the IRA were 'policed' by Sinn Féin stewards wearing orange armbands. Once inside the cemetery, I stood back from the republican plot where the burials were to take place, choosing a spot on high ground overlooking the scene as thousands of mourners poured into the graveyard and gathered in a mass around the plot. We knew we had at least one other crew positioned up ahead closer to the burial ground. Then, without warning, the sound of an explosion. We could see the puff of smoke. Then another explosion, another puff of smoke. There were screams. Mass panic. As mourners near the republican plot began to dive for cover we heard what sounded like gunfire. Then we saw him. A man with long unkempt hair and a goatee beard, wearing black gloves and what looked like a donkey jacket, moving slowly down the cemetery away from the republican plot towards the M1. This was Michael Stone. As I radioed our newsdesk to inform them of the scenes of panic and chaos, our cameraman locked in on Stone. At one point, after yet another explosion, Stone stopped. He raised a gun and fired back towards the pursuing crowd of mourners. Then he slowly turned to his right, his gun pointed in our direction. I ducked behind a gravestone and continued speaking to our incredulous office, my eyes fixed on the bomb-throwing gunman.

'Someone is throwing bombs and shooting in the cemetery,' I said. 'Listen.'

I pressed down on the microphone button and held the radio above my head. Peter Cooper kept the camera on Stone until he left the cemetery and disappeared from view along the M1 behind a factory building. One of our other crews had arrived by now and I asked them to take shots of the white van parked on the cemetery side of the M1, convinced that this was the fleeing gunman's means of escape. But as Stone got closer to the motorway, the van moved off. Once he was lost to view I got the tape out of the camera and ran to my car, parked near the gates of the cemetery. Within fifteen minutes of Stone's attack, pictures of the incident were being shown in the United States and Canada. I know this because a BBC executive from Belfast was in America at the time and called to say he had just seen the pictures.

Stone was lucky to survive. His two handguns had jammed, otherwise he would have been shot dead by the crowd that caught up with him. A police patrol arrived to rescue him from the beating he was receiving but his guns later found their way into the hands of the IRA. Stone admitted six murders and a catalogue of terrorist crimes going back to 1984. He told police he was a dedicated loyalist freelance and that he had seen the security files of those he said he had killed, describing them as legitimate targets – clearly implying collusion with members of the security forces in Northern Ireland. He said all his attacks had been, to use his word, 'sanctioned.' However, he later denied any involvement with the British Army.

Stone's attack generated a vicious spiral of violence, culminating three days later – during the funeral of IRA man Kevin Brady, who was one of the three killed by Stone – in the murders of two soldiers, army corporals Derek Wood and David Howes (who had arrived in Northern Ireland in the previous week). Again the police kept a discreet distance. The two soldiers had driven towards Brady's cortège. Their car was surrounded and the windows smashed, and the men were dragged out to be stripped and beaten before being driven off to waste ground and shot dead by the IRA. The images sent around the world in still photographs and on video tape were shocking. The sight of a priest, Fr Alex Reid, kneeling over the men's naked and beaten bodies to administer the last rites left an indelible impression. Throughout the history of the troubles, at least up until this point, television tended to sanitise its reports of the conflict but here we had emotive images of the last moments in the lives of two soldiers who were in the wrong place at the wrong time.

Now here I was visiting Stone in prison in 1989, on the first of several visits to see him. It was not the first time in my journalistic career that I had sat down face-to-face with a killer but it was the first time I had done so with someone whose killings I had witnessed. Like others I had met in the line of duty on both sides of the loyalist/republican divide, he was engaging, he smiled and told jokes. But his eyes held dark secrets.

During our second meeting, Stone told me that his targets that day were leading republicans Gerry Adams and Martin McGuinness, whose deaths had been, to use Stone's word, 'sanctioned' immediately after the Enniskillen bombing. He told me one of our crews had prevented an earlier strike as the cortège passed the Andersonstown Leisure Centre. They were directly in his line of fire, so he decided not to make the attack there. He told me he had received letters from young loyalists expressing admiration for what he had done, but that he wrote back to tell them not to follow his path in life.

He denied being on some kind of 'suicide mission', stating that self-preservation was a 'big thing with me.' But he would not be drawn on the subject of who, if anyone, was supposed to assist his escape.

The trial judge said Stone should not be considered for parole before thirty years had elapsed. Stone reckons he will never again walk free.

Someone else still coming to terms with what might have been described as a life sentence was Alex Ferguson, who had arrived at Old Trafford as manager in succession to Ron Atkinson in November 1986. As Michael Stone launched his murderous attack, United were riding high in the league, and in Ferguson's first full season in charge, we were coming close to winning the title. Maybe now, finally, we could put the frustrations of the 1980s behind us.

The decade had begun with United under the control of Dave 'Sideways' Sexton. His legacy comprised Joe Jordan, Gordon McQueen, Ray Wilkins and Gary Birtles, bought at £1,250,000. Sexton's successor, Big Ron Atkinson, immediately made it his business to rid the club of Birtles – selling him back to Nottingham Forest for a bargain-basement £275,000 after an undistinguished sixty-three games and just twelve goals. Not that Big Ron's exploits on the transfer market were always that positive. He had briefly on United's books one Peter Beardsley, purchased from Vancouver Whitecaps for just £250,000 after impressing with two great goals against United in a pre-season friendly. Beardsley arrived and departed during the 1982–83 FA Cup winning season. He made just one appearance on 6 October 1982 in a second round Milk Cup tie at home to Bournemouth, although he was substituted by an emerging star from Belfast, Norman Whiteside. Having just bought Bryan Robson for a record fee of £1,500,000 along with Frank Stapleton (£900,000), Remi Moses (£500,000) and John Gidman (£355,000), and having off-loaded Joe Jordan, Mickey Thomas, Sammy McIlroy, Jimmy Nicholl and Tom Connell, perhaps Big Ron was justified in thinking he had the makings of a championship-winning team. He never did manage that feat, but he came close (his team never finished outside the top four in the league) and he had the wonderful knack of getting to cup finals, even managing to win a couple.

Dave Sexton's term as manager ended on 30 April 1981 – just five days before the death of IRA hunger striker Bobby Sands. Before United appointed Ron Atkinson to replace him in July, another three hunger strikers had died, five soldiers had been killed in a land-mine attack at Bessbrook, County Armagh, two IRA men were shot dead by soldiers in Derry and tensions in Northern Ireland were running very high.

The delay in appointing Atkinson was explained by the fact that United's board had tried to recruit three others without success, Lawrie McMenemy, Bobby Robson and then Ron Saunders, manager of the new League Champions, Aston Villa. In Atkinson, United had chosen a manager in the 'Doc' mould, and with ability. By the spring of 1983 the team was heading to Wembley for two finals – the Milk Cup (our first ever appearance in the final of that particular competition) and the FA Cup.

The Milk Cup final against Liverpool on 26 March was the cause of some concern to me, given that it was being played on a day when I was expected to attend the wedding in Portstewart of BBC sound recordist Mervyn Moore. The match was to be broadcast live on television. I made sure we arrived in the town in time to go to a pub, called Spuds, I think, to watch the game. United were without three key players (Robson, Buchan and Gidman), yet after just twelve minutes the 'Boy Wonder' Norman Whiteside struck a marvellous goal to become the youngest player in the history of League Cup finals to score. Minutes later Kevin Moran was injured and replaced by Lou Macari. Then McQueen was hurt and pushed on to the wing as a passenger. Not for the last time in a Wembley final, Stapleton dropped back into defence. United held on grimly until the seventy-fifth minute when Alan Kennedy scored the equaliser and then in extra time Whelan won the cup for Liverpool with a stinging, curling shot.

Still, we were back two months later at Wembley in the final of the FA Cup. We drew the first game 2-2 with

Brighton but won the replay 4-0 on 26 May, Sir Matt's seventy-fourth birthday. Bryan Robson inspired us in the replay, scoring twice, but it was 'Roy of the Rovers' stuff for the young Norman Whiteside, who scored a cracking goal four minutes after Robson's opener. I watched the match in a bar in downtown Belfast, having had to slip out of a function nearby on the flimsy excuse of seeking out my own brand of cigarettes.

The two Wembley cup final appearances and a third place in the league augured well for the 1983-84 season, and throughout the summer of 1983 United supporters everywhere looked forward to the new campaign with optimism. On a personal level, that summer marked the end of my marriage after thirteen years. Renting a room in a house in the Castlereagh area of the city, I saw my three children briefly at weekends, work permitting – although at thirteen, Jason had begun to develop his own social life at weekends. We won four and lost two of our opening six games in the 1983-84 season. Our seventh game was against Liverpool at Old Trafford. We were fifth in the league but a 1-0 tanking of the Scousers in front of 56,121 spectators lifted us up to second, the winning goal coming from Frank Stapleton. The beer tasted good that Saturday night.

Next day I was the weekend duty reporter and as things were quiet I got permission from the duty editor George McEvoy to take a couple of hours after lunch to bring my two youngest children, Steven and Louise, to the swimming baths at Castlereagh. It was around 4.30 pm when I got them back to Carryduff. There was an urgent message waiting there for me to contact George at the office. The Sunday afternoon peace had been shattered by news of the IRA's mass breakout from the Maze Prison, in which a prison officer had been killed. To his eternal credit, George never squealed on me and I cut across country to cover the story, spending the next thirty-six hours in and around the Maze Prison gathering interviews with eyewitnesses and feeding material back to the office. A full decade later I would be interviewing the prisoners who planned and executed the escape for a *Counterpoint* documentary entitled 'Unlocking the Maze'.

Manchester United finished the 1983–84 season in fourth place in the league, but were knocked out of the Milk Cup in the fourth round by Oxford United and beaten in the third round of the FA Cup by lowly Bournemouth. But before our heads could drop too low in disappointment, the following season (1984–85) Big Ron provided us with another injection of success to keep us going for another year.

The new season got off to an indifferent start with the first four games drawn before we walloped Newcastle United 5–0 at Old Trafford and Coventry 3–0 away. That brought us to the home game with Liverpool which ended 1–1, a Gordon Strachan penalty for us. Our next game was away to West Bromwich Albion on Saturday 29 September 1984. That morning I was wakened from my slumbers by a telephone call from the office. It was around six o'clock. The Irish navy had intercepted the yacht the *Marita Ann* off the Cork coast with a load of weapons destined for the IRA. Network news in London wanted me to go immediately to Aldergrove Airport to meet the pilot of a small chartered plane who would fly me and the crew to

Cork. We took off about an hour and a half later and as soon as we touched down in Cork, our pilot made a few calls to mysterious contacts of his. We went straight back up in the five-seater plane, heading out over the sea in search of the *Marita Ann*, which was being escorted back to Cork by two Irish naval vessels. Amazingly, we soon had sight of the weapon-laden ship and our cameraman was busy taking whatever shots he could get through the small windows. We did not waste much time, deciding to head back to Cork to get the pictures on the air.

The BBC's London newsroom was delighted to hear that we had pictures of the ship under escort. They told me RTE was expecting me to transmit the pictures to London. We raced at full speed towards Cork city centre and soon I was at the doors of RTE. The commissionaire on duty telephoned someone, I assumed, in the newsroom. The deadline was approaching and after ten minutes I was beginning to panic. It seemed we had the first pictures of the *Marita Ann*. I went off down the corridor towards the newsroom and opened the door to an office where I heard voices. Three or four met sat around a table smoking and drinking coffee.

'Chris Moore, BBC,' I said. 'Where should I take this tape for transmission to the BBC in London?'

They were as calm as I was agitated. 'You're in the wrong place,' one said. 'You can't send it from here. You have to go to the transmitter up the mountain.'

Time was running out and I was unfamiliar with Cork city – this was my first visit! Armed with their directions, I set off at a run back to the car and eventually made it to the transmitter on the mountain. I knew I was late. The

RTE engineers rushed the tape to a machine. The BBC lunchtime news had kept going for an extra four minutes as they waited for my pictures. As the tape hit the machine, the news finished. For the first time I had missed a deadline.

I dreaded the call to the newsroom in London. They were very understanding but I knew I had failed. I felt hopelessly deflated. I had let BBC Northern Ireland down.

My instructions for the next day were to go to the small fishing village of Fenit in Kerry where the boat had berthed. We made that journey but could not persuade anyone to speak to us before we had to leave to make our next deadline. On the journey back towards Cork I noticed a convoy of Irish navy personnel in Ford Transit vans heading in the opposite direction. They all seemed to be wearing dress uniform, blue with white webbing and gloves. 'Where are they going?' I asked aloud. This was decision time. I had little to report from Fenit, so as we sat at traffic lights in Tralee watching the vans move off in the opposite direction, I instructed the crew to turn around and follow. They warned that I would miss the deadline – again! – but I decided to take the gamble. We followed for a few miles without knowing what was going on. Even when the navy vehicles made a 'pit-stop' the officers I approached would not tell me where they were going. I persisted and followed.

The Irish navy was providing the guard of honour at a ceremony a few miles north of Fenit, at Banna. The Republic's deputy prime minister Dick Spring was present to unveil a statue to Sir Roger Casement – the Irish patriot executed by the British for running German guns to Banna Strand on a ship called the *Aud*! This on the day after the

Irish government had intercepted the gun-running ship the *Marita Ann*. The irony was not lost on the small group of republicans who demonstrated at the ceremony with banners, demanding to know of Mr Spring and the government of which he was a part the difference between the *Aud* and the *Marita Ann*. Now I had a story. An exclusive, because no other television crew turned up, and funnily enough, for once the Irish government's press officers were not drawing attention to Mr Spring's engagement.

That day my hunch worked out but my hunch that United might now challenge for the league title proved to be little more than fantasy as the team again finished in fourth place. However, Big Ron got us back to Wembley in the FA Cup final against Everton. I had taken my elder son to a cup final in 1979 so it was only fair that my second son, Steven, by now ten years old, should have the same opportunity. He was not making any demands but had hinted very strongly that he would love to see United at Wembley. The game was to take place on 18 May 1985. Coincidentally, *Panorama* were planning a programme on John Stalker's investigation of RUC shootings in County Armagh in 1982 which had left six men dead – five of them unarmed members of republican paramilitary groups. I was due to travel to London to meet the *Panorama* reporter Peter Taylor and managed to arrange this for Friday 17 May. If only I could get tickets for the game. Getting two tickets proved to be a nightmare and I ended up buying them through the black market. This was a good move and a bad one at the same time. Good because it meant Steven would see United for the first time and, as with his brother Jason, the occasion would be an FA Cup final at Wembley. Bad because my black market tickets placed us at the Everton end of the ground, surrounded by Scousers of the blue hue! Nauseating or what?

There was no way we could disguise the fact that we were United supporters, given that I was bedecked in our colours, as was Steven – complete with a bloody big red-white-and-black flag purchased along Wembley Way. We had followed what was by now my traditional route to Wembley, via the pub in Notting Hill, mixing with the United lads who congregated there and travelling by tube to Wembley. At the top of Wembley Way our United chums headed off to the right side of the stadium while we were pointed in the other direction. Once inside, we were trapped among the less than friendly Scousers. Everton came to this game with the League Championship in their hip pockets, not to mention the European Cup Winners' Cup which they had won in Rotterdam three days earlier. So, just like Liverpool in 1977, Everton were chasing a 'treble' and, as with Liverpool, only United stood in their way. We had fucked up Liverpool's dreams of a three-trophy season – could we repeat it?

Everton began the game as hot favourites, even though United had disposed of Liverpool in the semi-final after a replay. United doggedly defended their goal against a classy Everton attack during the first, scoreless, forty-five minutes. Throughout the opening half, Steven and I were giving United the benefit of our vocal support – not that it was appreciated by the Everton fans behind us, particularly one group led by a punk with bleached blond hair, a Johnny Rotten type in Sex Pistols garb who kept throwing dirty looks in my direction. At half-time he went further and pissed down the terracing on top of our nylon overnight shoulder bag. I moved it away from the torrent and kept it on my shoulder for the remainder of the game. As the second half got under way, I asked the 'colourless' lads standing to my right if they might think about offering me and Steven some moral support by producing their colours and helping us sing. They did. At least we did not feel so isolated. Kevin Moran became the first player ever to be sent off in an FA Cup final, leaving us to face much of the second period with just ten men. As before, Stapleton dropped back into defence and his spirited performance gave us all a lift as United's defence held to full-time.

At this point I faced a dilemma. I had arranged for a taxi to meet us at the entrance to the Wembley Conference Centre to take us to Heathrow for the last flight back to Belfast. To miss it meant another night in London. I even suggested to Steven that we should leave, but, quite rightly, he told me to 'get real'. I understood. We stayed, and, well, the rest is history. United's ten men played their hearts out, moving more quickly to the ball and to the challenge. In the final moments of normal time they looked the better bet for victory. Extra time was like taking a downhill ride on a driverless Alpine bus – facing disaster at every corner, then miraculously steering away from sudden death.

The goal came at one of those moments when you sense something special is about to happen. 'Sparky' Hughes made a beautiful pass from midfield with the outside of his right boot, bending the ball away from the Everton defence into space on the right wing and into the path of the rampaging Big Norm. As the Belfast lad moved menacingly towards the Everton goal, I felt as if the world had stopped and fallen totally silent; and even though Big Norm was attacking the goal at the opposite end of the stadium I could hear the thump of his left foot on the ball. At that moment all the torment of the previous two hours ended. It took the ball an age to travel from Big Norm's left foot on its route around first, the oncoming tackler and second, the outstretched arm of Southall. And still there was silence and time stood still. Movement and noise were restored the instant the ball hit the corner of the Everton net. Six bodies surrounded by the despairing fans in blue jumped and hollered for joy, outstretched arms thrusting victorious fists towards the sky, the noise exaggerated by the silence all around us.

Suddenly we could feel the dagger looks of hatred coming from the blue-hue Scousers. My punk rocking chum was now making it quite clear that he wanted to cause me damage. Just when I should have been cowering in fear, the sheer ecstasy of the moment carried me through his venom. We watched the remaining moments of the game, but the terror of defeat was gone.

Once the final whistle blew, we moved towards the exit in the hope that the taxi driver might have waited for us. We were virtually alone descending the steps of the stadium. Halfway down I looked back. Johnny Rotten had emerged along with Syd Vicious and a handful of cronies. They glared in our direction. Now the elation of victory left me, replaced by the fear that these brave bastards in blue were going to start a ruck, attacking a ten-year-old boy. I moved Steven along with a shove in the back and told him to be ready to run.

'Why?' he asked in total innocence of the danger lurking behind. The punks were following. We picked up pace. They picked up pace.

'When I say run, you move as fast as you can to the place we were to meet the taxi,' I said to Steven. 'And don't ask why.'

We picked up the pace again, by now almost jogging. The Scousers did not respond, but continued their verbal assault. We kept moving, down more steps on to Wembley Way and the safety of numbers. With safety came defiance. I turned back to face the bitter Scousers and raised my right hand in a two-finger salute. We paused among the police officers and watched the sad Scouse bastards disappear from view. Of course the taxi had gone, so as we waited to join the United fans spilling out of the stadium, we made a call to British Airways and re-booked our flights for the next day. We also booked a room, and celebrated by taking in some of the sights of London.

During the spring and summer of 1985 I was busy along the shores of Lough Neagh researching the shootings John Stalker was investigating, and witnessing the street disturbances caused by the re-routing of Orange parades away from Catholic areas – away from what the Orange Order regarded as their traditional routes. This was the summer that the BBC decided not to transmit a documentary programme, 'Edge of the Union', which focused on Gregory Campbell of Ian Paisley's Democratic Unionist Party and on Sinn Féin's Martin McGuinness. BBC journalists throughout England, Scotland, Wales, Northern Ireland and the rest of the world were asked to strike for one day, 7 August, to voice their disapproval of this brand of censorship. As the father (shop steward) of the BBC chapel in Belfast I was deeply involved in organising our day of action. We found a way around the BBC's self-imposed ban. We hired a generator and wired up a television and video recorder on the pavement outside Broadcasting House in Ormeau Avenue. We played a video tape of the programme continuously throughout the twenty-four hours of the stoppage. News of our unorthodox transmission reached Derry and we soon had Gregory Campbell standing among the small crowd of onlookers. He told us he thought it was a fair programme and could see no reason for the decision not to transmit.

This was also the summer when I took my first holiday in the sun – Fiona and I joining our friend and fellow-journalist Tom Coulter and his wife Josie on their honeymoon. Well, we were asked to go! We spent four weeks on the Greek island of Spetses. From there it was a nightmare trying to follow United's performances at the start of the new season. The British papers arrived on Spetses a day late, but in most cases I knew the results by the time they arrived. The owner of the small cigarette kiosk where I used the telephone was utterly bemused by my celebratory antics – knees bent as if I had been shot in the back, then suddenly upright with a fist punching the air accompanied by a loud and extended: 'Yeeeeeeeeeeeeeeeeeeeeesssss!'

'Manchester United,' I would explain.

'Football, Englanders, brilliant,' he would respond.

Everybody had heard of Manchester United. This was the year Big Ron's team won their first ten games, sitting proudly on top of the heap. Five of the games were played

Gordon. I was in Enniskillen a few hours after the blast, interviewing anyone who would talk to me at the scene, at the hospital where more than sixty survivors were fighting for their lives, and later at the church services where clergymen of all denominations condemned the bomb makers for their 'barbaric' act.

A BBC radio producer from Enniskillen, Charlie Warmington, heard about Gordon Wilson's sad loss. He took his radio reporter Mike Gaston to see Mr Wilson at his home, and the interview with him was first transmitted after midnight on Radio Ulster. It was an extremely moving tribute from a father to his daughter. Charlie approached the family at my request to ascertain whether Mr Wilson could face a television camera. It is never easy to establish, without running the risk of harassment and invasion of privacy, whether someone from the family of a murder victim wishes to speak to the media. Gordon Wilson agreed to speak to us.

Charlie Warmington took us to his home. With me was n English crew recently arrived from London. We set up the living-room of the Wilson home, where I noticed a ture of Marie in a silver frame. The interview lasted over seven and a half minutes. I asked three ques- . In answering the second, Gordon Wilson dried up, le to speak. He had been describing how Marie had his hand as they lay among the rubble created by mb blast. As I watched this brave man struggle to is control, I almost lost mine. If he had broken would have broken down as well. Somehow he to continue, offering his forgiveness to those le for murdering his daughter and stating that

whilst we were speaking pigeon Greek. The kiosk man was more bemused than ever when news of the away game against the 'bitter blues' was delivered, courtesy of David Lynas, my Manchester United mate back home. Then came the war-dance of delight in front of startled holiday-makers and diners seated all around the picturesque harbour. It was a gift at 3-0.

But it was too good to last, and although we maintained our position at the top of the league right through to January 1986, United had begun to lose their way as far back as November. Many reasons have been offered for this but there is no doubt that a deal the club tried to keep secret was the principal cause of United's problems. While we had this wonderful opportunity to build on a stirring start to the season, a chance to end the title voodoo, the club had sold our best goal-scorer, Mark Hughes, to Barcelona for £2,200,000. They tried in vain to keep it a secret until the end of the season but it clearly had an impact on the player himself. The goals dried up and as a result there was no championship title. (Hughes, of course, was to return to enjoy a fabulous decade of achievement with United.) Nor were United's fortunes helped by the injuries to Bryan Robson, Big Ron's £2,000,000 signing from West Bromwich Albion, a player who was to give so much for United in the next ten years. But in this crucial season, he made just twenty-one appearances out of forty-two in the league. We finished fourth – again! The 1985-86 season was confirmation, if any were needed, that Big Ron was the 'Nearly Man' when it came to our league ambitions. As we sped towards the 1990s, his days in charge were numbered.

Of course, the end when it came was swift, the executioner's bullet rather than the assassin's poison. The date was 6 November 1986 – almost a year after the signing of the Anglo-Irish Agreement at Hillsborough Castle, an historic event which in one way or another dominated the political agenda from that point on, although it made little difference to the men with the guns and bombs, who carried on as 'normal'. As 'Ulster said No', and as Belfast's Lord Mayor Sammy Wilson was busy banning Northern Ireland Office ministers from attending the Remembrance Day ceremony at the City Hall, United's chairman Martin Edwards was returning to Manchester from Aberdeen, where he had travelled immediately after saying goodbye to Atkinson. There would be no painful delay on this occasion. Edwards was able to name Atkinson's successor a matter of hours after telling Big Ron that his day had come.

Aberdeen's Alex Ferguson was take over at Old Trafford with an impressive CV. Restricted resources had not prevented him from breaking the Old Firm hold on Scottish football by building an Aberdeen side which under his control had won three Scottish League Championships, four Scottish Cups and the European Cup Winners' Cup. Of course the cynics said his achievements were confined to the 'Mickey Mouse' Scottish League, overlooking completely the fact that a Scottish side was the first British team to win the European Cup, a team that had subsequently beaten the best English league soccer could throw at it in European competition.

Ferguson inherited a team lying second from bottom of Division One, but in that first year with no money to spend on buying the team's way out of trouble, he

brought the side to eleventh place in the league. He also introduced a tougher disciplinary code which immediately brought him into conflict with the likes of Paul McGrath, Norman Whiteside, Kevin Moran, Billy Garton and Gordon Strachan, all of whom were fined for transgressing Fergie's new rules. Perhaps most important of all was Ferguson's attention to the crumbling youth team policy, which should be the bedrock of any big club. We all know how successful he has been in this department. For eight months Ferguson spent nothing, then in one day he signed a goal-scorer and a defender. Twenty-three-year old Brian McClair came from Glasgow Celtic for £850,0[?] having scored thirty-five goals for the Celts in his [?]vious season. England fullback Viv Anderson was [?] from Arsenal for £250,000. Soon he moved to m[?] for Norwich City's central defender Steve Bruc[?] it turned out, at £825,000.

In Ferguson's first full season in char[?] when Manchester United finished second i[?] committed what might be considered [?] fanatics an act of treason. On 4 Augu[?] Fiona – a devout Liverpool supporter[?] back from our honeymoon on Spe[?] Ireland witnessed yet another of [?] which momentarily stunned so[?] country once more into the d[?] was a tragedy which would [?]

Nurse Marie Wilson wa[?] when an IRA bomb explo[?] gathered at the War Mer[?] Poppy Day wreath-la[?].

he would 'pray for those people tonight and every night'. We offered our condolences and left.

As we left Gordon Wilson's home, full of admiration for his spirit of forgiveness, the crew confessed that they too had almost broken down in tears at *that* moment. Reporters are often regarded as parasites who feed on the misery of the world, hard bastards who harass and harangue and invade the privacy of the bereaved. But none of us who have covered the events of nearly thirty years of murder and hatred can escape unscathed. My experience with Gordon Wilson was not the first occasion on which I came close to tears. Watching the dignity of widows as they bury their murdered husbands, or widowers paying their last respects to their murdered wives, has never been easy. But to see the pain of children who have lost a parent, trying to cope with their grief in public, is the worst of all. I have seen children – the daughter of a policeman in Moira one Saturday afternoon and the son of a hunger striker – crying out for their daddies, reaching out to touch the coffins in inconsolable grief.

Such was the impact of Gordon Wilson's interview on me that I resolved never again to intrude on his life. I wrote to him afterwards expressing my sorrow at his loss and my admiration for his courage. Other reporters asked me for his address or telephone number but I never gave it out. Sadly, Gordon Wilson has since passed away, but because he spoke to the media, his legacy will live on forever. The day I interviewed him was the only time we ever met, but it was not the last time I had to make that dreaded walk to the front door of a family recently bereaved. Gordon Wilson's Christian courage clearly had little impact on those who had the guns and the bombs. As we left the 1980s behind, there was little to suggest that the gunmen were ready to stop the killing.

At Old Trafford, Alex Ferguson approached the 1990s with little to show for his three years in charge. Indeed, some of the United fanzines were already losing patience, giving voice to the whisper that perhaps it was time for another change. But Ferguson was not anywhere near ready to quit. Two of the United fanzines, *Red Issue* and *United We Stand*, recently published an annual to mark their tenth anniversary. The title says it all: 'From Fergie Out to the Double Double'. Indeed! Bring on the 1990s!

PART IV

THE GLORIOUS NINETIES

8

FERGUSON'S RED-AND-WHITE ARMY

The K Stand members were giving it some trip! The whole stand vibrated as I surveyed the wondrous half-time sight of a packed Old Trafford from seat number 126 in Row 3. I was directly behind the goal into which Giggsy had scored a short time before with a superb free kick to level the game at 1–1. Having lived through the IRA's no-warning car bomb campaign of the early 1970s in Belfast, the vibration in the stand recalled to me the sensation of a bomb going off close by, except that now the shudder in the concrete beneath my feet was continuous. I felt myself being drawn out of my seat, down the steps towards the vast corridor just behind the stand where catering was provided for spectators, a journey I generally did not make because the crush inevitably meant missing the first few minutes of the second half as you struggled back to the seating area.

As I moved slowly down the steps towards the tea bars, what I saw was something I will never be able adequately to describe in words: a sea of humanity, thousands of faces, each of them fitted with a smile that stretched from ear to ear. All the faces were bouncing up and down in unison to the rhythm of some kind of trance-inducing Indian rain dance, the air heavy with the repeated chant, 'Champion-eeeees!' Even the cops on duty in the K Stand wore wide grins and had become part of the celebration, dragged into the joyous commotion by supporters who had, like me, waited almost twenty-six years for this day, Monday 3 May 1993.

In Old Trafford there were 40,447 spectators for the final home game of the season, against Blackburn Rovers. Even before they arrived at the Theatre of Dreams they knew that Manchester United had won the league title for the first time since 1967. It was an emotional gathering. Strangers looked each other in the eye and embraced with uncontrolled delight. Fists were thrust skywards in a gesture of defiance, eyes directed towards the heavens. The only word needed to accompany this tribal salute on such an occasion was: 'Yesssssssss!' Thousands filled the corridor, although few were bothering to purchase drinks of any description. Everyone was simply dancing on the grave of those twenty-six miserable years, the years dominated by the Scouse enemy, Liverpool Football Club, the major force in English soccer during the 1960s, 1970s and 1980s, a team that had managed to win league titles a record eighteen times, thirteen of those titles between 1964 and 1990.

We returned to our seats to regale the stadium with a variety of United songs during the second half. The party resumed behind and beneath us, the stand continuing to vibrate. The players tried to entertain a crowd which for the most part did not need anyone on the pitch. 'We are the Champions,' we sang (Freddie Mercury was probably spinning in his grave). Tina Turner's 'Simply the Best' got a turn or two. There was great delight in our renditions of 'Are you watching, Liverpool?' Then there was the anthem to the team and manager, accompanied by everyone embracing the nearest person, and bouncing up and down as we sang 'Ferguson's Red-and-White Army'. These were the only words of a song which had often been chanted mantra-style throughout the season for periods of up to fifteen or twenty minutes in the hope of lifting the players to even greater heights.

Later we relived these joyous scenes on television. Only then did we realise that Sir Matt Busby had tears in his eyes as he saw Alex Ferguson's team end the nightmare. We owe so much to Sir Matt. Songs about the Busby Babes feature even today in the supporters' repertoire, and English clubs also owe him a debt of gratitude for defiantly taking Manchester United into Europe against the wishes of the English football authorities.

Sitting next to me that May day in 1993 was my eighteen-year-old son Steven, an unwavering United fan since he was old enough to talk and to understand the dire consequences for him should he mention any other club. 'U-nite-ed!' was in his vocabulary before 'mummy' or 'daddy'. Somewhere else in the Theatre of Dreams was my elder son Jason, smiling, laughing and joking with other red fanatics. From our seats in the K stand, Steven and I marvelled at the scene before us and laughed ourselves through the second forty-five minutes as United moved towards a 3–1 win, the players even taking time to pause during play and wave at the adoring fans as their names were called out individually. As we left the ground I explained my role in this outstanding success for United. 'Steven,' I said, 'it is quite simple. The first time I have season tickets, United win the league. It's obvious.'

We drank the night away in the Tap bar at Timperley with Sean Connolly, who was my next-door neighbour in

Altrincham during the eighteen months I spent with the BBC in Manchester, first as a reporter on the BBC 2 sports investigative programme *On The Line* and latterly as the programme's deputy editor. I had moved back to Belfast in November 1992 but still travelled over for as many games as possible. This was a game not to be missed. It was an emotional night – tears, beers and every so often a quiet moment of reflection, as if trying to make time stand still, hoping this feeling of elation would go on for ever and praying that the victory was not a mirage, that we would not awaken next morning with the Scousers still holding top spot. We drank toasts to Ferguson, to the team collectively and to every player individually. My own toast, repeated over and over, was to Liverpool. Yes! But only that they in turn would now endure twenty-six years of the misery of defeat.

We had to travel to Liverpool next day to make the journey home, such was the demand for seats on planes to and from Manchester. Speke is a tiny, insignificant airport, considering the population of Liverpool. As we waited along with other happy United fans for our flight to be called, we talked excitedly about the future and at one stage even contemplated a mission to the gates of Anfield to express our support for the Liverpool manager Graham Souness, talk of whose dismissal had been widespread in the tabloid press

Back home in Belfast it took days for the head and throat to recover. The heart never will. The twenty-six year curse had ended in style, with a team which was the envy of the entire footballing nation. We did not know it then, but the squad assembled by Alex Ferguson was to become the dominant force in British football in the 1990s, not least because of the number of young players who were coming through the youth system. But perhaps the most crucial moment of the 1992–93 season came on 26 November 1992. It occurred in the privacy of Martin Edwards's office at Old Trafford. The United chairman was chatting to Alex Ferguson when he took a telephone call from the managing director of Leeds United, Bill Fotherby. The Leeds man asked if they could buy Denis Irwin. The answer – rightly – was no. Alex urged Edwards to ask if Eric Cantona was for sale. Amazingly the answer was yes. Within a matter of days Cantona was a United player. This unexpected but inspired signing was the single most significant act on the way to ending the twenty-six-year nightmare.

Supporters looked forward eagerly to Cantona's first appearance in our colours, which took place on 6 December 1992 at the Derby game with City at Old Trafford. The enthusiasm with which we greeted King Eric certainly staggered my neighbour in the K Stand. A few months prior to his début – on 6 September to be precise – we had mercilessly taunted the talented Frenchman. While Leeds supporters sang 'Ooh, Ahh, Cantona', we were shouting 'Fuck off Cantona'. That day we beat Leeds 2–0, Leeds, the team we had 'gifted' with the championship the previous season. The K Stand had become the 'vocal point' of the stadium, as reconstruction work had already begun on the demolished Stretford End terracing. My neighbour had seemed happy to join the singing masses as they verbally assaulted the Leeds forward line, picking on Cantona and Lee Chapman in particular. Now we were singing 'Ooh Ahh Cantona' with equal vigour. It was too much for him. Such was his disgust at our behaviour that he spoke to me for the first (and last) time all season: 'A few weeks ago we were singing fuck off Cantona!' I pointed out that that was before he had signed for us. 'So fucking what?' was his retort.

Cantona came on as substitute against the bitter blues, in a game we won 2-1 with goals from Paul Ince and Mark Hughes. The King had arrived and the fortunes of Manchester United were about to change. Ferguson had had his back to the wall until in 1990 a victory over Crystal Palace in an FA Cup final replay almost certainly saved his United career and set us off *en route* to success in Europe, in turn laying the foundation for our run of championship victories.

United's FA Cup win in 1990 coincided with a change in my fortunes at BBC Northern Ireland. In the first few months of the year, a team of English police officers headed by John Stevens, Deputy Chief Constable of Cambridgeshire, interviewed me several times about my report the previous August on leaked UFF (Ulster Freedom Fighters) documents which, they said, proved collusion between members of the security forces and loyalist paramilitaries. This was to be one of the most controversial enquiries in the history of the conflict. But it was a call from a contact in the security forces which introduced a dramatic change of direction for me. My informant had vital details about how MI5 had successfully blocked two police investigations into the scandal of sexual abuse at the Kincora Hostel in East Belfast, the story I had begun to investigate in 1980. When a researcher for the BBC 2 programme *Public Eye* got in touch with me about another Kincora-related matter, we soon established that there would be an interest in my new angle on an old story. The consequence was a four-month attachment to *Public Eye*. Before we continued with the necessary research, there were meetings with senior BBC editorial management. Director-General John Birt took a personal interest in the story and publicly praised my interview with Gordon Wilson at the time of the Enniskillen bombing. It was decided to transmit a one-hour special, twice the normal programme length. This meant that I spent long periods of time living and working in London.

United got to Wembley in 1990 by beating Nottingham Forest, Hereford United, Newcastle United and Sheffield United, all away games. The semi-final against Oldham Athletic was drawn 3-3 but United won the replay 2-1 after extra time. I was restricted to watching the games on television during this charge towards Wembley; even though I was in London it was impossible to secure tickets for the final against Crystal Palace. Palace's semi-final against the Scousers was a joy to behold; they triumphed 4-3. No one can ever accuse me of bias where Liverpool are concerned; I simply do not care who beats them!

After the 3-3 draw with Crystal Palace at Wembley on Saturday 12 May 1990, Ferguson dramatically dropped goalkeeper Jim Leighton for the replay the following Thursday night at Wembley. He chose instead Les Sealey, who had played just two games for Manchester United during the league campaign when we finished nine from bottom. We had taken Sealey on until the end of the season but after his performance in the 1–0 replay victory over Crystal Palace, Ferguson gave him a one-year contract.

The *Public Eye* Kincora special was transmitted on 1 June 1990. It brought an unexpected bonus, an offer of work in Manchester, on attachment. The BBC's attachment system offers members of staff an opportunity to work temporarily on other programmes or in different regions, even in different disciplines. The prospect of working for the sports investigative programme *On the Line* appealed to me, not only because it would take me to the city for which my football-loving heart yearned and where my ashes are to be scattered, but also because the intensity of covering the conflict in Belfast for nearly twenty years had had a draining effect. Working for *Public Eye* on the Kincora story had given me a taste of liberation from the conflict that divided my homeland and the attachment in Manchester for what was initially to be a six-month contract was a perfect opportunity to gain valuable experience in another field. As 1990 came to a close I was reporting on continuing violence in Northern Ireland, like the 'human bombs' used by the IRA on 24 October to kill six soldiers and a civilian in attacks on border checkpoints at Derry and Newry, but there was the comfort of knowing that I had something new to look forward to in the spring of 1991.

9

THE MANCHESTER YEARS

'Oh, Sparky . . . how did you miss that?' I screamed at the television set. It was Sunday 10 February, and United were at home to Leeds United in the first leg of the Rumblelows League Cup semi-final. 'Which one's Sparky?' asked four-year-old Naomi, pointing to players on the screen. That morning strict instructions had been issued that I was to be on my best behaviour while watching the game after Sunday lunch. Fiona did not want her sister's family to witness my usual 'excitable' television game performance, in which I would question the parentage of the opposition, the referee, and sometimes in moments of extreme agitation, even our own players. We won the game 2–1 but not before I lost my composure under extreme provoc- ation.

'Jesus Christ,' I yelled, 'how did he miss that?'

Quick as a flash, the four-year-old Sunday school pupil was at her mother's knee. 'Mum,' she says, 'does Jesus Christ play for Man United?'

The laughter defused any prospect of retribution for my bad language. and to this day Naomi has, like my own children, maintained her interest in Manchester United.

This televised win against Leeds at the Theatre of Dreams was followed by a superb 1–0 victory over the same team at Elland Road. Just as I was about to head for my new job in Manchester the Reds were in the final of the Rumblelows League Cup at Wembley against Second

Division side Sheffield Wednesday, who were guided by our former manager Ron Atkinson. Big Ron had the last laugh, his team beating us 1-0. More significant for us was our progression to the final of the European Cup Winners' Cup against Barcelona at Rotterdam.

My first assignment for *On The Line* in Manchester was an investigation into the financial affairs of Tottenham Hotspur. I worked along with Allan Sharpe, a Spurs fanatic who was to produce the story. My first priority was to make sure I got to Old Trafford for as many games as possible – back on the Stretford End. There was a real buzz of excitement at Old Trafford, despite the fact that we had lost our way in the League Championship, hovering around fifth or sixth place, and completing the season at sixth. But while I was enjoying the close proximity of Old Trafford, witnessing, for example, Ryan Giggs's first full game for the club against Manchester City on 4 May 1991 in which he scored the only goal, a development in Belfast was soon to intrude on my new life in Manchester.

We had completed filming the Spurs story and the editing was getting under way when word reached me that officers from the John Stevens police enquiry into loyalist collusion had called to see me at the BBC's Belfast office. They wanted to serve a summons for me to appear at Belfast Crown Court on 13 May to give evidence of my meeting with members of the UFF. My bosses in Manchester were not very pleased with this development because I had been busy preparing to travel to South Africa along with two producers to make a thirty-minute programme on the impact of the new South Africa on sport. I spent a week 'on the run' to frustrate the police but eventually their colleagues in London managed to serve the summons and the BBC in Manchester had to re-think their position. A colleague replaced me on the South African trip.

The one positive outcome of this disappointing development was that I was in Manchester to watch television coverage of the European Cup Winners' Cup final against Barcelona, which was played in Rotterdam. Few of my work colleagues were United supporters but they gathered in a pub to watch the game and to celebrate a wonderful victory by United. 'Sparky' Hughes scored both our goals – the second a superb volley from an acute angle. From being on the verge of a major campaign to have him removed from office, Fergie had pulled off a major coup in the space of just twelve months! I watched the European final two days after giving my evidence in Belfast. As things turned out, this was my last connection with the Belfast newsroom of the BBC where I had worked for twelve years. The offer of a job as deputy to the editor of *On the Line* for the next run of programmes meant I would be staying in Manchester for the following twelve months at least.

I spent the summer of 1991 with programme editor David Taylor preparing and researching suitable subjects for thirty-minute single-subject sports documentaries, while just over a mile away Alex Ferguson continued his preparations for building a League Championship winning team. The work David Taylor and I did proved to be largely in vain because of changes in BBC management and policy. Nevertheless, Fiona and I went back to Belfast for Christmas 1991 to pack for our move to Manchester after the New Year. Internecine warfare continued in BBC

Manchester into 1992 but Fiona and I settled into our new house in Altrincham, five minutes away from Old Trafford. I had become a regular at the Theatre of Dreams and managed to get my son Steven over from Belfast for the occasional game.

At one stage I decided to investigate the operation of touts at Old Trafford for *On the Line*. When United qualified for their second successive League Cup final against Nottingham Forest in 1992, I went to Old Trafford when the tickets went up for sale. Because I was attached to their membership scheme I was entitled to get tickets for Wembley, except that I would have been well down the line as I had an insufficient number of tokens on my token sheet. United operated a system of publishing numbered tokens in the match programmes with the worthy intention of rewarding the loyal supporters. But of course the system was open to abuse.

On this day, I watched as touts stood around the forecourt in front of the Munich clock, meeting potential clients in huddles. I approached the guy who seemed to be in charge. In his hands he had a couple of plastic shopping bags packed with red membership books like mine (obviously false), each with a completed token sheet. He said he could supply me with all I needed to go up to the ticket desk and purchase a ticket for the final. At the time I was standing in full view of the ticket office. I took two of the books from him, bought two tickets at face value from the ticket office and returned the book and token sheet to the tout – along with £60 for himself. He gave me a phone number where I could reach him (although it turned out that he was never there) as he had agreed to help me to explain how twenty people were making a living out of touting Manchester United tickets. He is still making his money at Old Trafford because I saw him there on 23 April this year (1997) using a mobile phone as crowds gathered for the European Cup semi-final against Borussia Dortmund. With development reducing ground capacity during the early part of the 1990s, there was considerable money to be made on the black market.

Fiona – who had come to Old Trafford a few times to see United and once to see Rod Stewart – travelled with me to Wembley on Sunday 12 April 1992 to use the tickets I had bought from the tout. We defeated Forest 1-0. Another cup but still no league title, although we were looking good to end our twenty-five years of torture. Four days after winning at Wembley we beat Southampton at home (1-0), then drew 1-1 away to Luton to go top of the league. The first setback came when Forest exacted revenge for that Wembley defeat by winning 2-1 at Old Trafford while our closest rivals, Leeds, won 2-0 at home to Coventry. They went top again. We could still win it if we won our remaining games, and we had a game in hand. But then came disaster.

As I drove to London on the evening of 22 April on my way to California on business, I listened to radio commentary on United playing away to West Ham. As I reached the outskirts of London, the final whistle blew. We had lost 1-0 but I knew we could still win the title if we beat Liverpool at Anfield four days later. Back in my hotel bedroom in Richard Nixon's hometown in California after a busy day's filming, I could not contain my anticipation and reached for a phone. I got my son Steven out of bed in the middle of the night only to hear that we had been stuffed 2-0 by the Scousers and that the league title had gone to Leeds United, surely the worst champions in the history of the league. I was so depressed and so incredulous that Alex Ferguson and the team had let their chance slip that I got very drunk on beer and vodka. It was during this mood of deep depression at yet another season's failure that I resolved to secure a season ticket when I got back to Manchester. Maybe I could change our luck!

That is exactly what happened: we won the newly established Premier League title in its first year, with the beginnings of a team gearing itself up for years of Liverpool-style domination of the English game. At last United supporters could walk tall, free of the burden of league failure. Twenty-six years of failure had been exorcised. We were on our way, and things were going to get better! But how could you better a league championship? By winning the Double.

Even before the euphoria of the 1992-93 Premier League Championship had faded in our hearts, United were speeding towards a marvellous Double in the 1993-94 season. At one stage it looked as if they might even bring off a unique treble, having reached the final of the League Cup at Wembley. As United played Villa on 27 March 1994, I was in North Dakota investigating a paedophile priest by the name of Brendan Smyth for UTV's *Counterpoint* programme. From my hotel in Langdon, near the Canadian border, I was frantically trying to secure an interview with a young man who had been abused by Father Smyth but I was also waiting anxiously for the right time to phone home to get the result.

In between the business calls on the story of the priest, I got in touch with Fiona. Disappointment again. We had lost 3-1. Fiona knew the score but had not been watching the game so I was on to Steven to get the match report. We had played well enough but had not got the breaks – that was his verdict. Andrea Kanchelskis had been sent off in the last minute of the game for handling on the line. Steven said he looked a sorry sight as he left the pitch. Villa scored from the penalty and to me, 4,000 miles away, it sounded as if the 3-1 scoreline flattered the winners. I consoled myself by thinking of the opportunity to win the Double. United had beaten Sheffield United 1-0 in Sheffield, then travelled to Norwich for a 2-0 win before defeating Wimbledon 3-0 away with wonderful goals from Cantona and Irwin. In the quarter-finals we beat Charlton 3-0 at Old Trafford, in spite of having Schmeichel sent off just before half-time when the game was scoreless.

Ferguson had made one major signing during the summer of 1993, when he bought Roy Keane from Nottingham Forest for £3,750,000. What an acquisition! This boy could play and seemed to have the energy to run all over the pitch. United had an awesome squad and the side which settled down for most of the season was: Schmeichel; Parker, Irwin, Bruce, Pallister; Ince, Keane, Cantona, Kanchelskis, Hughes and Giggs – with McClair, Sharpe and even Robson making significant contributions.

By this stage I no longer had season tickets, so it was mostly televised games for me, although Jason, a resident

of Warrington, was close enough to the action to become
my eyes and ears at Old Trafford, occasionally aided and
abetted by my other son Steven. They were at Wembley
for the FA Cup semi-final against Oldham on Sunday 10
April while I watched the game live on television in the
Lobster Pot bar in Burtonport in Donegal. Our Double
dreams appeared to be on the verge of ruin when Oldham
scored in the first minute of the second period of extra
time. The ABUs (supporters of Anyone But United) in the
bar whooped with delight and for a painful fourteen
minutes it looked as though we would miss the Double. I
felt in my heart that if we lost this game we would also
fail in the league campaign. With seconds left to go, Mark
Hughes scored one of the most spectacular volleys of his
career to save the day, and our blushes. I was not slow to
let the ABUs in Burtonport know how important this goal
was to United. We romped home in the replay, 4-1,
inspired by the return of our Russian winger Andrei
Kanchelskis. The final, against Chelsea, was set for 14 May
1994.

In the meantime United knuckled down to winning the
Premier League with a string of four wins and a draw in
our final five games – including a satisfactory 2-0 victory
over the bitter blues, with Cantona scoring both goals. The
title became ours on 2 May 1994, when we beat our
closest rivals 2-1 at Coventry. We had beaten Ipswich
2-1 at Portman Road the previous day, but still had to
play Southampton (2-0) and Coventry (0-0) at home. Then
it was on to Wembley – well, for me it was on to the BBC
Club in Belfast to face the wrath of the ABUs who would
gather there to cheer Chelsea.

We clinched the Double with ease in a 4-0 win over Chelsea. It was difficult to believe we had done the Double of Premier League title and FA Cup. Sadly, one man who would have savoured the moment was gone. Sir Matt Busby, our greatest ever manager, had died on 20 January 1994 at the age of eighty-four. What better way to mark his death than for his club to do the Double. Mind you, before his death he did witness our very poor performance in Europe, when we were knocked out of the European Cup in the second round by Turkish side Galatasaray. We may have won our second championship title in suc cession, but until we win in Europe, Busby's record stands supreme.

The 1994-95 season was a disappointment on a grand scale. It began indifferently enough, like the old days under Big Ron or Dave 'Sideways' Sexton, with a mixture of victories, draws and defeats. By the time we faced our main rivals, Blackburn Rovers, at their Ewood Park ground on 23 October 1994, I was touring New York, Boston and Washington with loyalist politicians who just ten days earlier had announced ceasefires by the UFF and UVF. We were still in New York when I phoned home to get the score. Blackburn had finished the previous season runners-up and were now regarded as a serious threat to our ambitions to win the Premier League title for a third year in succession. Jason had gone to the game in Blackburn that day and his news was a tremendous fillip for me: we had won 4-2, the goals coming from Kanchelskis (two), Hughes, and a penalty from Eric the King after Henning Berg had been sent off for foul play. One member of the loyalist group was delighted with my news of United's victory: Joe

English of the Ulster Democratic Party is a United supporter.

How I envied my son Jason, a regular at both home and away games, doing something I had only ever been able to dream of. He was living out my unfulfilled youth. Jason said the Blackburn coach trip was one of the best away games for United fans. 'When we arrived in Blackburn,' he told me, 'the cops boarded the bus and welcomed us to Blackburn. They even told us where there was a pub near the ground that welcomed visiting fans. They told us we would have no hassles there.'

Jason keeps me informed of the issues topping the agenda for United fans. At this time (1994) there was evidence of growing resentment towards the club, not the team, because of the manner in which its financial plans were being developed. Four days prior to the Blackburn game, Jason had been at Old Trafford for the European Cup game against Barcelona, drawn 2-2. Unlike the successful English league clubs in the 1970s, we were governed by 'new' European regulations which restricted teams to playing four foreigners. These severely hampered United's European ambitions because we had a fair sprinkling of Irish, Welsh and Scottish players on our books. Like me, United fans believed the team that won a national championship should be the team that played in Europe. The way the regulations were working meant that most sides needed to have two first teams, one for domestic competitions and another for the European games.

Jason went to Barcelona on 2 November 1994 for the return leg, travelling with the official United travel agency. There was resentment that United were trying to cut off supplies of tickets to other more experienced travel agencies to ensure they cornered the market and the profit from away games. As it happened, the trip to Barcelona was not only our worst ever performance in Europe – we were humiliated by a 4-0 defeat which I watched in abject misery in the Big House pub on the Ormeau Road in Belfast – but it turned out to be a journey of grim endurance for those who signed up to travel with United. 'We made a big mistake going to Spain with United,' Jason said. 'We got to Manchester Airport and had a few pints. There was no drink permitted on the plane and once we arrived at Barcelona airport we were taken straight on to a coach and transported to the stadium. We were herded in through lines of Spanish police and left for four hours before kick-off. Once we had spent twenty minutes marvelling at the size and lay-out of the stadium we had fuck all to do. No alcohol, just soft drinks and awful food – sandwiches from a barbecue – more like raw sheep in a bag!' More hours of standing around after the game before being herded back to the coach for the journey to the airport, then flying out in the early hours of the morning without even having had a chance to see the city.

The most desirable mode of transport to away games, in Jason's experience, is to go with the coaches organised by the United fanzines. 'They get you there in good time for a few bevvies,' he said. 'And there are a few places United fans really look forward to visiting. Wimbledon for one, because they have so little support it means genuine United fans can get tickets. These are the fans who stood on the terraces year in year out, but who are now being squeezed out of Old Trafford because of the club's policy of seeking middle class credit card holders as customers. Away games to Wimbledon are superb; it is really like a home game because there are so many of us.' Coventry is another favourite. 'We beat them 4-0 there and I don't remember seeing a goal, we were in such great form before the match. The Coventry fans are great.'

All-seater stadia have reduced hooliganism – not done away with it, just reduced it to an 'acceptable' level, in much the same way as there has appeared to be an 'acceptable' level of violence in Northern Ireland. Jason has travelled to away fixtures and experienced the type of hatred that sets off clashes between rival fans. 'There is still violence,' he says, 'it is just that it is organised differently now. The police and clubs tend to play it down because it happens well away from the grounds, but it happens when rival gangs arrange to meet somewhere for a digging match. They were trying to arrange something at Kilburn for the Chelsea cup final. Kilburn is where a lot of Chelsea fans hang out, apparently. At some grounds the police still escort visiting fans in and out because of the fears it will kick off . . . places like Newcastle, Liverpool and Leeds.'

In London the night before United's League Cup final with Aston Villa, Jason and a few other Manchester United fans were walking through Leicester Square just past Planet Hollywood when they realised that Villa fans in two pubs they had passed had recognised the Manchester accents. 'We were nearly surrounded and certainly out-numbered as they moved in on us,' he recalls. 'Our lot all moved to the other side of the street and I thought, well, if I remain on this side I should be all right. I saw one of the United boys turn on the pursuing Villa fans, lift the can out of a rubbish bin attached to a lamp post and thump a Villa fan who was ahead of his mates. The guy just fell on his back, his head thumping against the pavement. For a moment I thought he was dead. The United boys then ran off, pursued by Villa fans. Some tourists looked on, terrified. One of the Villa lot saw me loitering outside a shop window and accused me of being one of those Man United bastards. I told him I didn't know what he was talking about. Then a couple of other Villa bastards broke away from the main body and turned towards me and this other bloke. I walked past him, pushing him and saying I hadn't a fucking clue what he was on about. Once clear of them I legged it for all I was worth.'

Earlier that same day, Liverpool had been in London for a game against Arsenal which they lost 1–0. Jason and a group of United fans were having a pint at around half past five in the evening when the publican closed and locked the doors. He had received a tip-off that a group of pissed Scousers were on their way around to start trouble. A short time later, thirty to forty Scousers walked by, singing and yelling, obviously looking for somebody to fight.

Of course I worry about Jason at away games, but I would be there myself if circumstances permitted so I have to trust he will look after himself. He does not endorse violence but he says it is hard to stay calm at times, such as when rival fans hum the *Dambusters* tune and raise their arms to imitate an aeroplane, a clear reference to the Munich disaster. There was the visit of Sheffield Wednesday to Old Trafford, for example: 'They had the K stand and they all stood doing the Munich thing during the game. They started letting the Wednesday fans out at the same time as us, for some reason. I saw men with kids waiting behind to have a pop at those bastards. It was sad to see the kids being terrorised but there was no justification for the Wednesday fans to refer so cruelly to Munich. The United boys got stuck into them. The same thing happened for one of Chelsea's visits. They do it to provoke so they have to accept the consequences.'

Getting back to the 1994–95 season, the next time Eric the King faced Blackburn was on 22 January 1995 at Old Trafford. In this game he scored the only goal. No one knew it at the time, but it was to be his last full ninety-minute game for United until October. In his next outing, away to Crystal Palace on 25 January, Cantona's temper snapped after he had been sent off and he let fly with that famous Kung-Fu kick at a Palace fan. When the pictures came on the news that night I just could not believe what I was seeing. Of course, next day all the anti-United brigade at work were quick off the mark with jokes about the incident and demands that Cantona be banned for life. Once the hysteria had died down and Eric had his prison sentence reduced to community service on appeal, we got on with trying to win the Double for the second successive season. We failed on both counts.

We had a new striker in Andy Cole, bought suddenly and unexpectedly from Newcastle United where he had been a tremendously prolific goal-scorer, but in my opinion he is not a great player. I watched him closely in one particular game for Newcastle and was less than impressed with his skill on the ball. Ferguson paid Newcastle £6,000,000 and threw in the Northern Ireland right-winger Keith Gillespie, who in his short time in the first team squad had become a big favourite with fans. Keegan must have been laughing all the way to the bank. I liked the way he stood on the steps outside the offices at Newcastle's ground and confronted angry supporters, telling them that it was a move made in the best long-term interests of the club. But Cole has always left me cold. I still view him as a flawed signing and nothing he has done has convinced me that he will ever come good.

Cole made his United début against Blackburn at Old Trafford, the side he had last played against for Newcastle in a 1-1 draw in the FA Cup at St James's Park. He played no part, therefore, in our cup run to the final against Everton, and to my admittedly biased view, he failed to do his business in the last league game of the season at West Ham when we had to win and Blackburn had to lose away to Liverpool. We drew 1-1, and Cole missed at least one good chance. Surprisingly, the Scousers did us a favour by beating Blackburn, but it was to no avail – the title was Blackburn's by one point.

FA Cup day was Saturday 20 May 1995. My plan was to leave home in the early hours to travel to Sligo to play golf with three friends, watch United stuff the Scousers, spend the night getting pissed and play golf on the Sunday and Monday. Domestic difficulties meant I could not travel on the Saturday morning as planned, so it was Saturday evening before I could meet the other three in Bundoran. However, the delay meant I was at home when the postman called, delivering the first half-dozen copies of my book, *Betrayal of Trust*, about the Father Brendan Smyth affair. Down at the BBC Club I took all the shit they had to throw in my direction as United lost to Everton 1–0. A lousy end to a lousy season.

Then came what appeared to be our summer madness. The world – myself especially – thought Alex had lost his grip on reality when, during the summer of 1995, he had a clear-out! Rather than buy to strengthen the squad which had almost delivered the second Double in successive seasons, Alex chose to off-load Andrei Kanchelskis, Mark Hughes and Paul Ince, who had by now developed into the fiercest midfield competitor in Europe, a man who had arguably been our player of the year in the previous two seasons.

Saturday 19 August 1995. United away to Aston Villa. The team: Schmeichel, Neville P., Irwin, Parker, Neville G., Pallister, Butt, Keane, McClair, Scholes, Sharpe. Subs: Beckham, O'Kane. Result: Aston Villa 3 Man. Utd. 1. Cut to BBC's *Match of the Day* studio after recorded highlights of this embarrassing start to the season where that Scouse 'expert' Alan Hansen is providing the nation with the benefit of his 'wisdom' about the game. Hansen's inadequacies as an objective commentator were exposed when he came face to face with Rudd Gullit during the Euro '96 tournament. The Dutchman slaughtered him with the clinical accuracy of his predictions, his assessments and his knowledge of the game. The worst of the rubbish Hansen came out with can be summed up in the following remark about Manchester United: 'You can't win anything with kids!'

The 'kids' went on to win not only the Premier League but the FA Cup! The Double Double! The first team ever to acquire such a collection of silverware. And to think it was the Scousers we stuffed in the Wembley final to clinch the FA Cup, the second half of the second Double! Such sweet retribution! Thanks anyway, Alan, for the benefit of your expertise. I now wear the words 'You can't win anything with kids!' on a T-shirt along with the Manchester United symbol. Underneath that is recorded the following: 'FA Carling Premier League Champions 1995–96. FA Cup Winners 1995–96. The Double Double.' Before the season was over, the 'kids' emerged with great dignity and adulation as well as the main trophies. Beckham became an English international, along with the Neville brothers. Cantona returned from his suspension for the eighth match of the season at home to Liverpool – drawn 2–2. He led his motley crew of youngsters like any good captain, and for good measure he was chosen as Footballer of the Year by the Football Writers.

We beat Newcastle home and away and had the pleasure of see that other former Scouser Kevin Keegan completely discredit himself live on Sky TV Sport when he attacked Alex Ferguson, barely able to articulate his argument for the venom he was spitting out at the same time. Keegan and Hansen, two former Scouse players who are held up to the public gaze as experts from 'Anfield University'. They should have been there to help out the less fortunate, like Souness and Evans!

10

IN GOOD FAITH

Moments earlier 54,000 spectators had packed the Theatre of Dreams to witness our sad exit from the European Cup with our third home defeat in the competition. About 5,000 supporters remained, singing our hearts out at the 3,500 Borussia Dortmund fans on the other side of the lines of stewards and coppers. This cultural exchange lasted for nearly an hour after the final whistle and was punctuated by moments of sportsmanship when both sets of supporters paused to applaud a handful of the German players who were cooling down on the Old Trafford pitch. I stood beside my son Steven glorying in this unique moment. We applauded them. They applauded us. We even had the Germans joining in some of our songs. We sang: 'If you all hate Scousers clap your hands!' They clapped. They sang: 'Man-chest-ter, la la la!' We applauded. When we had finished, we met up outside under the watchful eyes of hundreds of police officers as we exchanged souvenirs – shirts, scarves and badges.

Our favourite song on this sad night of European defeat was: 'We won the Football League again, this time on Merseyside, this time on Merseyside, this time on Merseyside.' This was a reference to our team's magnificent performance four days earlier at Anfield when we tanned the Scousers 3–1 in front of their own supporters. It virtually finished Liverpool's challenge for this year's league title, leaving us five points ahead of them and

Arsenal with a game in hand and requiring only five points from the remaining four games, three of those games at home. Premature? No doubt. A formality? Let us hope. Borussia's 1-0 win on 23 April meant that the league is our only hope of a trophy, a trophy that will, with any luck, be back at the Theatre of Dreams for the fourth time in five seasons by the time this book hits the shelves. Given our start to the season, we should be thankful for small mercies. So for a moment, let me reflect on the dark days of last October.

'Five-nil, six-three and one-nil last night,' said the sneering face right into my gob at the doorway of the UTV works canteen on a dreary Thursday morning. It was 31 October 1996 to be precise. It was the third time in ten days that I had been compelled to walk the gauntlet of ABU abuse. 'Fuck off,' I sneered back, 'sure your team hasn't even managed a point in Europe yet!' Bloody Rangers fan! Then there's Frank Mitchell the weatherman – a Manchester City supporter. 'Shit on the City, Shit on the City tonight!' His lot could barely win a game in Division One, had just sacked their manager Alan Ball and were so desperate to find a replacement (what with all the refusals they had from the likes of George Graham, Dave Bassett, Kenny Daglish and Mother Theresa) that they were spotted loitering with intent outside Moss Side Job Centre. And what about poor Stevie Coppell? Thirty days of playing Old Mother Hubbard to an empty trophy cupboard was obviously too much for someone accustomed to winning with Manchester United. And Frankie boy finds time to poke fun at us, he and all the other sad souls who delight in United's misery. No need to mention that I too delight in seeing Liverpool, Leeds, Arsenal and Manchester City losing match after match.

Alex Ferguson and the lads, I am sure, had their own difficulties to face after losing 5-0 to Newcastle United on 20 October (with Kevin smiling on the bench), 6-3 to Southampton six days later and then the biggest disappointment of all, losing to Turkey to ruin a forty-year record of no European defeats at Old Trafford, the Theatre of Dreams. It was threatening to become a Theatre of Nightmares. Of course, even after defeat, no, *especially* after defeat, I invite abuse because I insist on wearing my United colours. No one will accuse me of being a fair weather supporter. Every day, somewhere on my body there is a symbol of the greatest club team in the universe. When we get beaten I brace myself for the worst. The Newcastle hammering was a disaster waiting to happen.

The week before the great Geordie disaster, on 12 October, I travelled to the Theatre of Dreams for the home game against Liverpool. I occupied seats I share with two Belfast-based season ticket syndicates and even though we were played off the park in the second half we managed to hold on to the 1-0 half-time lead. The goal was a brilliant strike from the edge of the box from David Beckham but beautifully set up by the baby-faced assassin, Ole Gunnar Solskjaer. This kid is one of last summer's signings and he has control and movement reminiscent of the great Denis Law. He will, I predict, achieve great things with United. Now he has his own song to the tune of 'You Are My Sunshine':

You are my Solskjaer, my only Solskjaer,
You keep me happy when skies are grey,
You cost no dearer than Alan Shearer,
Please don't take my Solskjaer away.

That win over the Scousers was to be our last league victory for some time. Four days later we travelled to Turkey to beat Fenerbahce SK 2-0, but other results simply did not go our way. Our return from Turkey heralded that slump in form starting with the 5-0 hammering by the Magpies, which soon had the office ABUs cracking jokes about the Manchester United crisis line – telephone 0891-5-0-6-3-1-0! They overlooked a couple of wins sandwiched in between these results, like a 2-1 win over Swindon in the Coca Cola Cup ... and dare I mention the little acknowledged 3-0 win over Norwich at Carrow Road on Monday 11 November, in a testimonial match for Norwich goalkeeper Bryan Gunn.

This worrying run of misery began at St James's Park, Newcastle. Five-nil! I left my sister's house after a good lunch to watch that game at home alone as she does not have Sky Sports. For a few minutes on that dismal Sunday afternoon, time was suspended. That first goal from Peacock was definitely a goal. It crossed the line all right but it should have been booted clear before it got there. I would have had time to walk the dog (if we had one) between the ball being headed goalward, then moving snail-like over the line before one of our defenders finally lunged at it. At 1-0 down, the game was still retrievable but it was one of those days when things simply did not go our way. Newcastle got revenge for the Charity Shield

4–0 hammering in August at Wembley. I watched in abject misery as the game moved on towards that drubbing, the first time, incidentally, that any team managed by Alex Ferguson had suffered such a heavy loss. Already I could see the gloating faces of the ABUs at the office.

Next day, into work, the MU scarf draped very visibly around my neck, and time to run the gauntlet of ABU abuse from what seems like everyone in the workforce from management down. That walk is all of forty yards through the UTV newsroom and on a day when everyone is at their station (aren't they always after a United defeat?) it is a formidable dander. Let me talk you through it. Most likely the first to catch your eye is the sports department on the right. There's Adrian Logan the Nottingham Forest fan, Des Fahey (Celtic), Bruce McKendry (Arsenal), Steven Watson (Liverpool and Rangers), and immediately opposite them on the left hand side of the room is the 'bubble-blower' himself, Mike Nesbitt (West Ham United). Once through this crowing quartet you are most likely next to see Frankie boy (Manchester City). Directly opposite Frank there's big Ivan Little, a Linfield supporter, so we don't have too much difficulty with his lot at the moment. Finally, if he hasn't caught me at the news editor's desk, our head political honcho and deputy news and current affairs editor Ken Reid. Now here's a fine example of a 'blue' Scouser, those Everton toffees who stuck one on us in the 1995 cup final.

The Monday after the second of our run of defeats (6–3 at Southampton), there was a great buzz of excitement when I entered the newsroom. Reid, McKendry, Logan, Nesbitt and Watson were all screaming for me to 'wait a moment.' One of them was dispatched in great haste towards the editing booths. It was Nesbitt who returned clutching a tape close to his chest. As he thrust it into the machine they all gathered around (along with a few 'civilians' come to watch). There was a deathly hush as we all waited to see what was coming up on the screen. And then, two soldiers playing 'The Last Post' on bugles. Amid howls of laughter all round, the quivering quintet then stood to attention, saluting and laughing uncontrollably. Can't say I blame them: they have had so little excitement in their lives for years with Everton, Arsenal, Forest, West Ham and Liverpool. So if they can overlook the shortcomings of their own teams and celebrate my misery, at least some good has come from our bad form.

Ignoring their taunts, I predicted that we would win the league. There was a new confidence about the way Alex Ferguson was handling affairs at Old Trafford. He had created a team that was dominating the domestic game, in spite of its shortcomings in Europe. For twenty-six years we had to endure Liverpool's success in the league. Now it was our turn to enjoy domination. We supporters had followed United through the good times and the bad. For nearly four decades my life has revolved around United's achievements. Even as I lived through twenty-five years of murder and destruction there has always been a part of me that could divorce itself from the sad reality of the suffering all around in order to celebrate our successes and mourn our defeats.

Even defeat brings its own enjoyment because there is a choice to be made – either take the jokes with a pinch of salt or join in the rough-and-tumble of the verbal assaults. I prefer the latter. Verbally 'eyeballing' opposition fans was the very thing that generated atmosphere at football matches. Mingling with the masses on the terraces you didn't know if your neighbour was a mad axeman or a bank robber. You were united by location and by the team colours you wore. These were sufficient grounds for comradeship; you were warriors together against whoever was on the terraces opposite.

Football terraces provided an outlet, an opportunity to get rid of all the tension built up during the working week. The rivalry was tribal and on occasion it could create an almost tangible hatred in the air but for all that I really enjoyed the cut and thrust. At Old Trafford today, the kind of people who sit down to watch the game do not have it in them to create any atmosphere. There may be 55,000 in the stadium, but you can hear the change rattling in somebody's pocket at the other end of the ground, a point not lost on United's manager Alex Ferguson who urged fans to: 'Stand up, stand up for the Champions!' He wanted the fans to play their part in making Old Trafford a noisy cauldron, to strike fear into opposing teams. The fans responded and the result was a marvellous atmosphere during the Juventus European Cup game. But the problem for Ferguson is that having got the supporters on their feet in an all-seater stadium, he could not get them to sit down again. There have been almighty rows between fans wanting to do the best for their club and the club stewards who are under orders to make people sit down.

At the FC Porto game, Steven and I managed to stand and sing throughout the match without any trouble. The entire sections of supporters behind each goal remained on their feet throughout. Then at the Borussia game Steven and I had difficulties with some nearby supporters who had no desire to contribute to the performance of their team, playing in their most important fixture for nearly thirty years, with a place in the final of the European Cup at stake. We wanted to stand and shout and sing, just to make a noise to help the team, but there was limited response until the final fifteen minutes when everyone in the stadium finally stood and cheered. What an experience! What a racket! But why wait until it was almost too late? United beat Porto against all the predictions of the ABUs and undoubtedly the crowd contributed to their performance. Against Borussia, the team attacked and should have scored at least four (two were disallowed). Had there been sufficient noise at the beginning, maybe the result would have been different.

United fans have been urging the club to create a singing section where all those who want to roar and yell for ninety minutes can do so without causing arguments with people in the row behind. But in the letters sent out just before the game with Borussia the club says it cannot for safety reasons permit such a development:

> To maintain our capacity and avoid the very real possibility of the most stringent sanctions we really do need all supporters to remain seated throughout the match except, of course, for those moments of extreme excitement when supporters will instinctively stand, if only momentarily. It will be a great shame if we are forced to cut down our capacity

and possibly withdraw season tickets in order to prevent what is now rightly seen as a major problem. In the light of these concerns, it is felt inappropriate to introduce a singing section at the present time.

In the official United club magazine of May 1997, chairman Martin Edwards addresses the issue in an interview, quoting the law which states that football stadia must be all-seater. He expresses regret at the loss of atmosphere and admits that he would happily allow some standing areas, not as large as the big Kops of old, but smaller areas in front of seating. Now that Labour have won the election, let us hope that they will honour their pledge to re-examine the issue of terracing at football grounds, and maybe we can get the singers at Old Trafford into a huddle to enhance the team's performances on the pitch. Edwards rightly points out that no one who saw the pictures from Hillsborough would want to return to that type of risk.

The Hillsborough disaster changed attitudes to safety on terracing. Watching the recent television dramatisation of the story was a very moving experience. It was easy for me to identify with all those people who could not contain their delight at getting hold of FA Cup semi-final tickets, unaware they were walking into a death trap. In Jimmy McGovern's excellent script the fans and their families talked about being treated like cattle by the police, and I knew exactly what they meant. However, as things stand, the working class terrace supporter has lost his place. He feels disenfranchised and alienated by the credit card Americanisation of English football. For many faithful United supporters, the only way to get into a game these days is by saving up to buy a ticket from a tout. This is a real issue which demands urgent attention from clubs, football's administrators, the police and other authorities if the game is to regain the atmosphere of old, without the hooliganism and risks to safety.

Meanwhile I look forward to the 1997–98 season. We have youth on our side. The future is *red* with the natural born winners! Yes, there is only one team in Manchester – and its name does not rhyme with shitty! Next year as the bitter blues remain in Division One I will mourn the six points we are normally guaranteed but rejoice in the hope that after this year's experiences in Europe we will go on to win the European Cup. To do that, we need to buy a more reliable goal-scorer than Andy Cole. Ferguson has already begun the search. Had Shearer come to us, we would have made it to the European Cup final in Munich. The game would have been played in the Olympic stadium on 28 May 1997 – the stadium built for the ill-fated 1972 Olympics and constructed on the site of the old airport where the great Manchester United team died on 6 February 1958. And that thought brings us back to the beginning . . .

POSTSCRIPT: 6 MAY 1997

Manchester United are Premier League champions 1996–97
yet again, for the fourth time in five years!

Natural Born Winners
The Team of the Decade

We won the football league again
This time on Merseyside.

THE GREATEST UNITED TEAM – EVER

Every supporter dreams of watching his or her club's eleven all-time greats competing against the top sides in a cup final or League Championship, mixing past heroes with stars from the present. As I never saw the pre-Munich Busby Babes in action, my selection is flawed because it is based entirely on written works which extol the virtues of Manchester United sides in the mid- to late 1950s. However, as someone who has followed the Reds through the 1960s, 1970s, 1980s and 1990s, why should I not daydream a little about the greatest ever United XI? (The statistics for those players still playing are valid up to the end of the 1995–96 season.)

Peter Schmeichel
Denis Irwin, Gary Pallister, Duncan Edwards,
Tony Dunne
Eric Cantona, Bobby Charlton, Roy Keane
George Best, Denis Law, Ryan Giggs

Substitutes
1 Harry Gregg; 2 Pat Crerand; 3 David Beckham;
4 Norman Whiteside; 5 Mark Hughes; 6 Steve Bruce

Peter Schmeichel (ex Brondby; £550,000; August 1991)
His arrival at Old Trafford coincided with the birth of a team which finally began to believe in itself, and the number of clean sheets he has kept has been a vital factor in making his United team a major force in European football. He had twenty-two clean sheets in the Double-

winning 1995–96 season, not to mention those mind-bending saves in one-on-one situations. Brilliant shot stopper, reads the game well. Many goal-scoring moves come from his superbly accurate throws. Remember his stunning one-man show against Newcastle at St James's Park in 1995–96, which laid the foundation for a 1–0 win with Cantona's goal. By far the most consistent, confidence-inspiring keeper we have had since Harry Gregg. Eighty-seven caps for Denmark.

Dennis Irwin (ex Oldham; £625,000; June 1990)

Mr Dependable. Excellent record since joining us. A top-class athlete who misses few games through injury. Reads play well and even though he can be a little slow on the turn, he more than adequately compensates by his timing and tackling qualities. Solid at right or left back. Free kick specialist (who will ever forget that cracker against Liverpool in the famous 3–3 draw?) until the emergence of Cantona and Beckham. Pity. Should still be given the occasional opportunity. Forty caps for Republic of Ireland.

Gary Pallister (ex Middlesborough; £2,300,000; August 1989)

A colossus in defence who has dominated United's penalty area ever since he joined in 1989. Tremendous pace – apparently he is the fastest of our players over sixty yards from a standing start – and that is not bad when you consider he is up against the likes of Ryan Giggs! United have struggled in defence when he has been injured. His first few seasons he was virtually injury-free but has had a worrying back problem in the last two seasons.

Duncan Edwards (joined United from school)

Made his début for United at just sixteen and was an England international two years later. Never saw him play, but many respected commentators have had the privilege of witnessing his swashbuckling style and have rated him one of the greatest individuals ever to wear United's colours. He was destined for world status before Munich robbed international football of a true genius. He died on 21 February 1958, sixteen days after the crash. As Munich survivor Bobby Charlton once said: 'If I had to play for my life and could take one man with me, it would be Duncan Edwards.' Tremendous ball control with both feet, his shooting accurate and powerful, fantastic in the air and read the game better than many more mature players.

Roy Keane (ex Nottingham Forest; £3,750,000; July 1993)

The first of several players purchased from Nottingham Forest to make the grade. The Corkman is versatile in defence or midfield and has an uncanny ability to sneak in an occasional crucial goal. His energy and commitment make him outstanding although he is prone to moments of sheer madness, probably because he goes on to the pitch knowing he would die for the United cause. Comfortably took control of midfield when Paul Ince left. Shades it over Ince because of his versatility. Thirty caps for Republic of Ireland.

Eric Cantona (ex Leeds Utd; £1,200,000; November 1992)

Le Dieu. The most influential, inspirational and naturally gifted player to grace Old Trafford in a United shirt since George Best. A talisman who lifted the team and the fans to new heights of achievement, who on the pitch single-handedly broke the Scousers' hold on the League Championship, not just with his own contribution as a player but also as a wonderful inspiration to United's young players. The captaincy has helped to stabilise his volatile temperament. When they write the history of Manchester United the name of Eric Cantona will be to the forefront alongside Best, Law and Charlton. Now this season he has finally freed himself of suspension to make his mark in the European Champions League. He has taken us to the Double Double. Forty-five French caps.

Ryan Giggs (from trainee)

Sitting at pitch level is the only way to appreciate the speed with which Giggs covers the turf. I was one of the 45,000 at Old Trafford on the day the seventeen-year-old Giggs made his début (Saturday 4 May 1991), scoring the winning goal in a 1–0 victory over City. Being sheltered by Alex Ferguson during those early days has not done him any harm at all. Giggs, now just twenty-two, is maturing with every game. His performance at home this season against FC Porto was his best ever in a United shirt. His wing play has been exemplary but his true potential is apparent in his stunning displays at midfield. Sixteen Welsh caps.

Bobby Charlton (joined United from school)

No United fan could choose a team without one of the greatest players in world football history. Bobby Charlton survived Munich as an eighteen-year-old with potential and emerged from the disaster as a man with tremendous match-winning leadership qualities. He was at home on the wing, in the middle as a striker, or in central midfield. My first United hero. His shooting ability terrified goalkeepers from Rochdale to Rio de Janeiro. His goals during the 1966 World Cup (against Mexico and Portugal) kept the English in the tournament. Strikes from twenty or thirty yards were regular features of his staggering 247 goals in 752 games for United. 106 caps for England.

Denis Law (ex Torino; £115,000; August 1962)
When he joined United in 1962 he had the same kind of impact as that which accompanied *Le Dieu*. Six minutes into his first game he scored the first of twenty-three league goals. Although the team struggled in the league, just avoiding relegation, Law led it to victory in the 1963 FA Cup final against Leicester City. He could hold the ball up, dribble with it and score amazing goals from all angles and distances. Scoring with overhead kicks was not uncommon; his scissors kicks were thrilling to watch. Law was the King, the original people's champion. I was one of countless thousands who took to wearing football shirts in the Law fashion – the cuffs pulled down over the palms and the hands closed to keep them there. His record of 236 goals in 393 games is a magnificent testimony to the King's abilities. Fifty-five caps for Scotland.

George Best (joined United from school)
At his peak the world's greatest player. It is a great pity he did not grace the game for at least another ten years. In the eleven seasons he played at Old Trafford George Best provided more memories of stunning brilliance than other players managed in twenty-year careers. In those years he was an integral part of the vintage attacking 1960s side, becoming European Footballer of the Year in 1968, also taking the British Player of the Year award that year. On his day dazzling, inspiring and oh, what an entertainer! Difficult to spot any flaws in his game. He could tackle hard, could take punishment, had mesmeric dribbling skills and was a natural athlete. Thirty-seven caps for Northern Ireland.